You’re Worth the Work

Choosing Yourself, One Day At a Time

By. C. Michael Welsh

This book is intended for informational and inspirational purposes only. The author does not provide medical, psychological, or legal advice. Readers are encouraged to seek professional guidance where appropriate.

First Edition

ISBN: 978-1-964122-41-0

Published by **The Change Maker**
thechangemaker.biz

All reflections and perspectives shared in this book are based on the author's personal experiences and insights unless otherwise noted.

Printed in the United States of America

Foreword

There comes a moment—sometimes quiet, sometimes undeniable—when you realize you can no longer keep living the way you’ve been living.

Not because everything has fallen apart,
but because something within you is asking for more.

More honesty.
More presence.
More alignment with who you truly are.

You’re Worth the Work was created for that moment.

Not the moment when everything is figured out,
but the one where you begin to see that something needs to change—and that you might be the one who has to choose it.

This is not a book about perfection.
It is not about getting everything right or becoming some ideal version of yourself.

It is about the quiet, consistent decision to show up.
To look at what’s there.
To stay, even when it would be easier to turn away.

Because choosing yourself is not always loud or dramatic.
Most of the time, it looks like small decisions.

Setting a boundary when it feels uncomfortable.
Saying no when you would have once said yes.
Pausing before reacting.
Taking a breath instead of numbing out.
Trying again, even after you’ve fallen back into old patterns.

Choosing Yourself, One Day At a Time

This work is not easy.
It asks you to be honest in ways you may not have been before.
It asks you to let go of what is familiar, even when it no longer serves you.

But it is worth it.

Not because it leads to a perfect life,
but because it leads you back to yourself.

Some days will feel steady.
Others will feel uncertain, heavy, or even discouraging.
That does not mean you are doing it wrong.
It means you are in it.

This book is meant to walk with you through all of it.

Each reflection is an opportunity to pause, to check in, and to choose—again—how you want to show up. Not just for the world around you, but for yourself.

You do not need to do this all at once.
You do not need to have all the answers.

You only need to be willing to begin.

And to remember, on the days you forget:

You are worth the work.

Opening Statement

Before you begin, pause for a moment.
Take a breath.
Not one you have to force — just a natural breath,
the kind that reminds you that you are here.

This book is not asking you to have it all together.
It is not asking you to be healed, certain, or confident.
It is only asking you to show up.

Wherever you are right now is enough.

These pages were written for real life.
For the days that feel clear and steady,
and the days that feel heavy and uncertain.
For the moments when you feel strong,
and the moments when you question everything.

There is nothing wrong with where you are.

You are not behind.
You are not broken.
You are not too far gone.

Each reflection in this book begins with a simple intention —
FOR MY GROWTH TODAY — because change does not happen all at once.
It happens in small, intentional choices made in today.

Not yesterday.
Not tomorrow.
Just here. Just now.

You do not need to read ahead.
You do not need to have a plan.

Choosing Yourself, One Day At a Time

Simply allow the words to meet you where you are.
Take what resonates.
Leave what does not.

This book is not meant to push you into becoming someone else —
it is meant to support you in choosing yourself.

For your growth today, begin here.

You Are Allowed to Begin Again

Somewhere along the way, many of us learned to believe that starting over meant we failed. That if we had to try again, heal again, trust again, or rebuild again, it somehow meant we were weak or broken.

But life does not move in straight lines.

Healing is not linear.
Growth is not linear.
Becoming is not linear.

There will be seasons where you feel strong and certain, and there will be seasons where you feel like you are learning the same lessons all over again. That does not mean you are going backward. Sometimes it simply means you are being given another opportunity to choose yourself more fully than before.

You are allowed to begin again after heartbreak.
After disappointment.
After addiction.
After grief.
After fear.
After losing yourself in places and people that could not hold the weight of your spirit.

You are allowed to wake up one ordinary morning and decide:
"I want something different for my life."

Not because you suddenly became perfect, but because somewhere deep inside you remembered that your life still matters.

Choosing Yourself, One Day At a Time

Beginning again does not require permission from the world. It only requires willingness. A willingness to take one more step. One more healthy choice. One more honest conversation. One more moment of believing that your future does not have to look like your past.

There is courage in choosing yourself when you once abandoned yourself to survive.

There is courage in trying again.

And maybe today is not about having everything figured out. Maybe today is simply about placing your hand over your heart and remembering that no matter how many times life has humbled you, there is still something sacred within you asking not to be given up on.

For today, let this be enough:
You are allowed to begin again.

Choosing Yourself in the Quiet Moments

Sometimes choosing yourself will not look dramatic.

It will not always be the big breakthrough, the life-changing decision, or the moment everyone around you applauds. More often, choosing yourself happens quietly — in the small moments no one else sees.

It is choosing to rest instead of pushing yourself past exhaustion.

It is drinking the water, taking the walk, saying the prayer, turning off the phone, going to bed earlier, or speaking to yourself with a little more kindness than you did yesterday.

It is deciding not to return to the places that continually emptied you.

It is learning that peace is more valuable than chaos that feels familiar.

Many people think transformation arrives all at once, but most lasting change is built through small choices repeated consistently over time. A life changes little by little before it changes all at once.

There will be days when your progress feels invisible. Days when healing feels slow. Days when you wonder if the effort is even making a difference.

Keep going anyway.

The quiet choices matter.

<u>Choosing Yourself, One Day At a Time</u>

The nights you stay committed to yourself matter.
The mornings you get back up matter.
The boundaries you set matter.
The tears no one sees matter.
The moments you choose growth over self-destruction matter.

You do not need to become a completely different person overnight to change your life. You only need to keep returning to yourself, one decision at a time.

Over time, those decisions become habits.
Those habits become identity.
And that identity becomes the life you once prayed for.

For today, remember this:
Your healing is not built only in the big moments. It is built in the quiet ones too.

Stop Waiting to Feel Ready

There are dreams sitting quietly inside people who have spent years waiting for the "right time."

The right time to go back to school.
The right time to heal.
The right time to leave what no longer fits.
The right time to start creating, living, loving, growing, or believing in themselves again.

But readiness is often misunderstood.

Many of the most important decisions you will ever make in your life will happen while you still feel uncertain. Courage is not the absence of fear. Courage is deciding that something matters more than the fear you feel.

If you wait until you feel completely ready, you may wait forever.

Growth stretches people.
Healing stretches people.
Dreams stretch people.

There will almost always be a part of you that wonders:
"What if I fail?"
"What if I can't do it?"
"What if I'm not enough?"

But there is another question worth asking:
"What happens if I never try?"

So many people quietly abandon themselves before life ever truly has the chance to meet them. Not because they lacked potential, but because fear convinced them they needed certainty before movement.

Choosing Yourself, One Day At a Time

You do not need absolute certainty to take the next step.

You only need enough willingness to move forward anyway.

Maybe readiness is not something you find before beginning. Maybe readiness is something that grows within you because you began.

The version of you that can carry the dream may not fully exist yet. That version is built through the process itself.

One assignment at a time.
One hard conversation at a time.
One boundary at a time.
One brave decision at a time.

You are becoming someone every single day, whether you realize it or not.

For today, remember this:
You do not have to feel fully ready to begin becoming the person you were meant to be.

You Do Not Have to Carry Everything Alone

Some people become so used to surviving that they forget they are allowed to receive support.

They become the dependable one.
The helper.
The listener.
The strong one everyone leans on.

And after a while, they stop reaching for others altogether because they convince themselves that needing help is weakness.

But human beings were never meant to carry the full weight of life alone.

Even the strongest hearts grow tired.
Even the most independent people need rest.
Even the people who encourage everyone else sometimes need someone to sit beside them and say, "You do not have to do this by yourself."

There is strength in vulnerability.
There is strength in honesty.
There is strength in admitting that something hurts, that something feels heavy, or that you are still healing from things you rarely speak about aloud.

Support does not always arrive loudly. Sometimes it comes through a conversation that reminds you to keep going. Sometimes it comes through prayer, friendship, recovery, community, therapy, family, or simply one person who sees your humanity beneath the mask you wear for the world.

You are not failing because you need support.

Choosing Yourself, One Day At a Time

You are human.

The truth is, many people spend years trying to prove they are self-sufficient while quietly starving for connection. But healing often grows best in safe spaces where we no longer feel pressured to pretend we are okay all the time.

You deserve spaces where you can exhale.

You deserve relationships that do not require you to perform strength every moment of the day.

You deserve support that feels safe, honest, and reciprocal.

And perhaps one of the bravest things you can do is allow yourself to be cared for without guilt.

For today, remember this:
You do not have to carry the weight of your life alone to prove that you are strong.

Becoming Someone You Can Trust

One of the deepest forms of healing is learning how to trust yourself again.

Not the version of you that acted from fear.
Not the version of you that abandoned your needs to keep the peace.
Not the version of you that kept returning to what hurt because it felt familiar.

The version of you that is learning.
Growing.
Awakening.
Choosing differently.

Self-trust is not built through perfection. It is built through consistency.

It is built every time you keep a promise to yourself.
Every time you follow through.
Every time you choose honesty over avoidance.
Every time you protect your peace instead of betraying yourself for temporary comfort or acceptance.

Many people spend years searching for safety in other people while feeling disconnected from themselves. But there is something powerful about becoming someone your own heart can rely on.

Someone who listens when their body says it is tired.
Someone who pays attention to what feels aligned and what does not.
Someone who no longer ignores red flags, intuition, exhaustion, or emotional pain simply to avoid disappointing others.

Trusting yourself again may feel unfamiliar at first.

Choosing Yourself, One Day At a Time

Especially if you spent years doubting your instincts.
Especially if life taught you to second-guess your worth.
Especially if survival required you to disconnect from your own needs.

But healing slowly reconnects you to yourself.

You begin noticing what drains you.
What nourishes you.
What inspires you.
What hurts you.
What brings peace.
What no longer belongs in your life.

And little by little, you stop needing everyone else to tell you who you are.

You begin building an inner relationship rooted in respect instead of criticism.

The relationship you have with yourself shapes every other part of your life.

For today, remember this:
Every healthy choice you make is helping you become someone you can trust again.

Not Every Season Is Meant to Be Shared

There are seasons of life that grow best in private.

Not because you are hiding.
Not because you are ashamed.
But because some things need quiet in order to take root.

A seed does not announce its growth while it is still beneath the soil.

There is wisdom in protecting certain dreams while they are still becoming. Sometimes sharing too early invites opinions, projections, comparison, or energy that interrupts the sacredness of what is trying to grow within you.

Not everyone will understand your vision.
Not everyone will share your excitement.
Not everyone is meant to have access to every part of your journey.

And that is okay.

You do not owe the world constant updates in order for your progress to be real.

Some of the most meaningful transformations happen quietly:

- in the early mornings,
- in the late-night studying,
- in the therapy sessions,
- in the prayers no one hears,
- in the boundaries no one sees,

- and in the small daily decisions to keep choosing yourself again.

There is a difference between seeking connection and seeking validation.

When you become deeply connected to your own purpose, you no longer need applause to continue walking toward it.

You begin understanding that your life is not a performance. It is a relationship between you, your spirit, and the future you are slowly building.

And one day, people may look at the life you created and wonder how it happened.

What they will not see are the quiet seasons that made it possible.

The unseen discipline.
The healing.
The restraint.
The consistency.
The faith.
The moments you kept going without recognition.

Protecting your peace is not selfish.
Protecting your dreams is not selfish.
Protecting your becoming is not selfish.

For today, remember this:
Not every season of growth needs an audience.

Your Life Is Not Behind

It is easy to look around and feel like everyone else is arriving somewhere before you.

Someone else is getting married.
Buying the house.
Starting the family.
Building the career.
Finishing the degree.
Finding the success.
Living the life you thought you would already have by now.

And if you are not careful, comparison will convince you that your life is somehow late.

But life is not a race with one universal timeline.

People bloom in different seasons.

Some people find themselves early.
Some people spend years surviving before they ever truly begin living.
Some people must lose who they thought they were before they discover who they were meant to become.

Your path may not look conventional.
That does not mean it is wrong.

There are lessons you learned through heartbreak, recovery, struggle, reinvention, grief, and growth that cannot be taught inside perfect timelines. The parts of your story that sometimes make you feel delayed may actually be the very experiences shaping your wisdom, compassion, and depth.

You are not behind because your journey looks different.

Choosing Yourself, One Day At a Time

You are not behind because you had to heal.
You are not behind because you changed directions.
You are not behind because you are still becoming.

Some dreams arrive later because you needed time to become the version of yourself capable of carrying them well.

And perhaps that timing is not punishment.
Perhaps it is preparation.

There is no expiration date on growth.
No age limit on purpose.
No deadline on becoming more whole.

You are allowed to evolve at your own pace.

The world often pressures people to measure their lives by milestones and appearances, but fulfillment cannot be measured that way. A person can appear “ahead” externally while internally feeling deeply disconnected from themselves.

Real success is not simply arriving somewhere.
It is becoming someone you are proud to live with along the way.

For today, remember this:
Your life is unfolding in its own time, and you are not behind.

Let Yourself Outgrow What No Longer Fits

Growth can feel uncomfortable because it often asks you to release things that once felt familiar.

Old habits.
Old identities.
Old relationships.
Old environments.
Old ways of coping and surviving.

Sometimes people cling to what no longer fits simply because it once made them feel safe. Even pain can become familiar enough to mistake for home.

But there comes a point in healing where staying the same begins to hurt more than changing.

You may notice yourself pulling away from conversations that drain you.
You may stop finding comfort in chaos.
You may begin craving peace, depth, honesty, and alignment more than attention or approval.

That is growth.

Not everyone will understand the changes happening within you. Some people only know the version of you that existed before your healing began. And sometimes, when you evolve, it changes the dynamics of relationships that were built around older versions of yourself.

That can feel lonely at times.

But outgrowing what no longer aligns is not betrayal.
It is self-respect.

Choosing Yourself, One Day At a Time

You are allowed to change your mind.
You are allowed to want more for your life.
You are allowed to stop shrinking yourself to remain digestible to people who are uncomfortable with your growth.

Healing often creates distance between you and the things that once kept you stuck.

And while there may be grief in releasing certain people, patterns, or places, there is also freedom in no longer forcing yourself to fit where your spirit has already outgrown.

Trust the discomfort that comes with becoming.

A new life often requires a new relationship with yourself.

The goal is not to become better than others.
The goal is to become more honest about who you are and what your soul truly needs to feel alive.

For today, remember this:
You are allowed to outgrow anything that no longer honors the person you are becoming.

Rest Is Not Something You Have to Earn

Many people were taught to believe that rest must be deserved.

That you must finish everything first.
Achieve more first.
Push harder first.
Prove your value first.

So they keep going long after their body, mind, and spirit have begun asking for care.

They wear exhaustion like a badge of honor while quietly losing connection with themselves.

But rest is not weakness.
Rest is wisdom.

Your body was never designed to exist in constant survival mode. Human beings need pauses. We need moments of stillness, reflection, recovery, and restoration.

Without rest, even beautiful things begin to feel heavy.

Sometimes the most healing thing you can do is slow down long enough to hear yourself again.

To breathe.
To pray.
To sit in silence.
To sleep.
To laugh.
To spend time in nature.
To reconnect with the parts of yourself that productivity cannot measure.

Choosing Yourself, One Day At a Time

The world will often reward overworking while ignoring burnout. But a life built entirely around constant output eventually becomes disconnected from joy.

You are more than what you produce.

Your worth is not measured by how exhausted you are. Your value is not determined by how much you sacrifice yourself to keep everything moving.

There is nothing lazy about caring for yourself.

Rest allows clarity to return.
Creativity to return.
Compassion to return.
Presence to return.

And often, the version of you that emerges after genuine rest is far more grounded than the version of you that kept forcing yourself to run on empty.

You do not have to abandon yourself in order to be successful.

For today, remember this:
You are allowed to rest without guilt.

The Life You Want Will Be Built by Small Decisions

People often wait for one big moment to change their lives.

A breakthrough.
A miracle.
A perfect opportunity.
A sudden transformation.

But most meaningful change happens much more quietly than that.

A life is shaped by small decisions repeated consistently over time.

The choice to keep showing up.
The choice to speak more kindly to yourself.
The choice to save money instead of chasing temporary comfort.
The choice to go for the walk.
The choice to stay sober.
The choice to study after a long day.
The choice to set a boundary.
The choice to begin again after a setback.

These moments may seem insignificant while they are happening, but over time they become the architecture of an entirely different life.

Many people underestimate the power of consistency because consistency rarely feels dramatic. It feels ordinary. Repetitive. Slow.

But slow progress is still progress.

Choosing Yourself, One Day At a Time

A healthy life is not usually built in giant leaps. It is built through daily decisions that gradually shift the direction of your future.

One healthy choice may not seem life-changing.
But hundreds of healthy choices over months and years absolutely are.

And perhaps one of the most important things to remember is this:
you do not have to become everything overnight.

You are not failing because you are still learning.
You are not failing because growth takes time.
You are not failing because your transformation looks gradual instead of immediate.

The strongest foundations are often built slowly.

There will be days when motivation disappears.
Days when discipline feels difficult.
Days when you question whether the effort is worth it.

Keep choosing your future anyway.

One day you will look around and realize that the life you once hoped for was not created through one perfect moment, but through many ordinary moments where you decided not to give up on yourself.

For today, remember this:
Your future is being shaped by the small decisions you make today.

Stop Apologizing for Wanting More

There is nothing wrong with wanting more for your life.

More peace.
More stability.
More healing.
More purpose.
More honesty.
More growth.
More fulfillment.

Somewhere along the way, many people learned to downplay their dreams so they would not make others uncomfortable. They learned to minimize their ambition, silence their needs, or shrink their vision in order to appear humble, agreeable, or safe.

But there is a difference between humility and self-abandonment.

Wanting to grow does not make you selfish.
Wanting a healthier life does not make you ungrateful.
Wanting deeper relationships, meaningful work, financial stability, emotional peace, or personal transformation does not make you "too much."

You are allowed to desire a life that feels aligned with who you are becoming.

The problem is not that people want more.
The problem is that many people chase "more" while disconnected from themselves. They pursue status without peace, achievement without balance, or validation without fulfillment.

But when your desire for more comes from a place of healing and alignment, it becomes something different.

Choosing Yourself, One Day At a Time

It becomes a willingness to stop settling for survival when you know you were created for deeper living.

You do not have to apologize for:

- going back to school,
- changing your habits,
- protecting your energy,
- building a better future,
- taking care of your health,
- creating boundaries,
- or becoming more intentional with your life.

Growth often requires you to outgrow old narratives about what you are allowed to want.

You are not here merely to exist through your days disconnected and depleted. You are allowed to create a life that reflects your values, your healing, and your evolving sense of purpose.

And the people who truly love you will not fear your growth. They will want to see you thrive.

For today, remember this:
You do not need to apologize for wanting a healthier, fuller, and more meaningful life.

Healing Does Not Always Look Beautiful

There are days when healing feels inspiring.

You feel hopeful.
Clear.
Motivated.
Connected to your future.

And then there are days when healing feels messy.

Days when old memories return unexpectedly.
Days when you feel emotionally exhausted.
Days when grief resurfaces.
Days when you question yourself, your progress, or whether you are truly changing at all.

This is the part many people do not talk about.

Healing is not always graceful.

Sometimes healing looks like crying in your car after holding yourself together all day.
Sometimes it looks like sitting quietly in a chair praying for strength.
Sometimes it looks like canceling plans because your nervous system needs rest.
Sometimes it looks like taking one healthy step while still feeling afraid.

Progress is not erased simply because you are having a hard day.

People often imagine healing as becoming endlessly positive or emotionally unaffected. But true healing is not the absence of emotion. It is learning how to move through emotion without abandoning yourself.

Choosing Yourself, One Day At a Time

You can still be healing while feeling overwhelmed.
You can still be healing while feeling uncertain.
You can still be healing while carrying grief, fear, disappointment, or exhaustion.

There is no perfect way to heal.

Some wounds close slowly.
Some lessons repeat until they are fully understood.
Some parts of you will need gentleness for far longer than you expected.

Be patient with yourself.

You are undoing patterns that may have existed for years.
You are learning new ways to think, cope, communicate, love, and live.
That takes time.

Do not compare your healing to someone else's outward appearance. Many people look fine externally while silently struggling internally.

What matters is not perfection.
What matters is your willingness to keep returning to yourself with honesty and compassion.

For today, remember this:
Healing is still healing, even when it feels messy.

The Way You Speak to Yourself Matters

There is a voice inside you that you hear more than anyone else's.

The way you speak to yourself shapes how you experience your life.

Some people move through the world carrying an inner voice that is constantly criticizing them:
"You're behind."
"You'll never change."
"You always mess things up."
"You're not good enough."
"You should be doing more."

After enough time, harsh self-talk begins to feel normal. People become so used to judging themselves that they no longer realize how deeply it affects their confidence, nervous system, relationships, and ability to grow.

But healing requires learning a new relationship with your inner voice.

Not a dishonest voice that pretends everything is perfect.
Not empty positivity.
Not denial.

A compassionate voice.
An honest voice.
A grounded voice.

Choosing Yourself, One Day At a Time

A voice that says:
"You are learning."
"You are trying."
"You made a mistake, but you are not a mistake."
"You are allowed to rest."
"You are still worthy while becoming."

The words you repeat internally matter because your mind and body are always listening.

You would likely never speak to someone you love with the level of cruelty you sometimes direct toward yourself. Yet many people spend years carrying shame-filled narratives that quietly drain their spirit.

You do not become stronger by constantly tearing yourself apart.

Real growth is built through accountability paired with compassion.

There is a difference between:
"I need to do better,"
and:
"I am worthless unless I do better."

One leads to growth.
The other leads to shame.

Changing the way you speak to yourself may feel unnatural at first, especially if criticism has been your default language for years. But over time, gentler self-talk creates safety within yourself.

And safety creates space for transformation.

For today, remember this:
Speak to yourself in a way that helps you keep going, not in a way that makes you want to give up.

Some Chapters Are About Rebuilding Yourself

Not every season of life is meant for constant expansion.

Some seasons are about rebuilding.

Rebuilding your health.
Rebuilding your confidence.
Rebuilding your finances.
Rebuilding your peace.
Rebuilding your relationship with yourself.
Rebuilding after loss, heartbreak, burnout, addiction, disappointment, or years of simply surviving.

And rebuilding can feel frustrating because it often requires slowing down long enough to strengthen the foundation before moving forward again.

There may be moments when you look at your life and think:
"I thought I would be farther along by now."

But rebuilding is not failure.
It is preparation.

A weak foundation cannot sustainably hold a meaningful future.

Sometimes life asks you to pause not because your journey is over, but because certain parts of your life need care before the next chapter can truly support you.

This can be difficult in a world that constantly encourages people to move faster, achieve more, and appear successful at all times.

But there is wisdom in rebuilding intentionally.

There is wisdom in learning:

- how to manage your money differently,
- how to protect your peace,
- how to regulate your emotions,
- how to care for your body,
- how to create healthier relationships,
- and how to stop abandoning yourself in the process of trying to build a life.

A rebuilding season may not always look impressive from the outside.

It may look quiet.
Simple.
Slow.
Private.

But internally, something powerful is happening.

You are becoming more stable.
More aware.
More grounded.
More aligned.

Do not underestimate the importance of seasons dedicated to repair.

For today, remember this:
Rebuilding yourself is still progress, even when it happens slowly and quietly.

You Are Not Meant to Abandon Yourself for Love

Many people spend years trying to earn love by becoming smaller versions of themselves.

They overextend.
Overexplain.
Overgive.
Overcompromise.

They ignore their intuition.
Silence their needs.
Accept behavior that hurts them.
And slowly disconnect from who they truly are in order to maintain connection with someone else.

But love that requires you to abandon yourself is not healthy love.

Real love does not ask you to betray your spirit to keep someone comfortable.

You should not have to constantly prove your worth to be treated with care.
You should not have to shrink your voice to avoid conflict.
You should not have to sacrifice your peace in exchange for attention, validation, or temporary closeness.

There is a difference between healthy compromise and self-erasure.

Healthy relationships allow room for honesty, individuality, boundaries, growth, and mutual respect. They do not require one person to carry the emotional weight of the entire relationship while neglecting themselves in the process.

Choosing Yourself, One Day At a Time

Sometimes people remain in painful dynamics because they fear loneliness more than disconnection from themselves.

But there is a loneliness that exists inside relationships too — the loneliness of not feeling seen, valued, emotionally safe, or fully accepted for who you are.

Healing teaches you that being chosen by someone else means very little if you are constantly abandoning yourself to maintain the connection.

The goal is not simply to be loved.
The goal is to experience love without losing yourself.

And often, the first step toward healthier relationships is strengthening the relationship you have with yourself.

Learning your worth.
Learning your needs.
Learning your boundaries.
Learning what peace feels like.

Because when you truly begin valuing yourself, you stop settling for relationships that continuously ask you to betray your own well-being.

For today, remember this:
You are worthy of love that allows you to remain fully yourself.

You Can Be Proud of Yourself and Still Be Growing

Some people struggle to acknowledge their progress because they are too focused on how far they still want to go.

They minimize their accomplishments.
Dismiss their healing.
Ignore how much they have survived, learned, and rebuilt.

They keep moving the finish line and rarely pause long enough to recognize who they have already become.

But growth and gratitude can exist together.

You can still have goals while being proud of yourself.
You can still be evolving while honoring your progress.
You can still desire more for your life without constantly feeling inadequate in the present.

There is nothing arrogant about recognizing your own growth.

In fact, learning to appreciate your progress is an important part of healing. When you only focus on what is missing, you overlook the quiet victories that are already changing your life.

The healthier choices.
The boundaries.
The discipline.
The honesty.
The sobriety.
The resilience.
The willingness to keep trying when life became difficult.

Choosing Yourself, One Day At a Time

These things matter.

Sometimes progress looks dramatic.
Other times it looks like becoming calmer in situations that once overwhelmed you.
Responding differently.
Choosing peace over chaos.
Staying committed to yourself even when motivation fades.

Not every transformation will be visible to the outside world, but invisible growth is still real growth.

You are allowed to pause and acknowledge:
"I have come a long way."

Not because the journey is complete, but because the version of you reading these words is already different from the version of you that once felt hopeless, disconnected, afraid, or uncertain.

Becoming takes time.

And perhaps one of the kindest things you can do for yourself is stop treating your current self as unworthy simply because you are still growing.

You are already becoming someone worth being proud of.

For today, remember this:
You do not have to wait until you are fully healed to appreciate how far you have already come.

Peace Will Sometimes Feel Unfamiliar at First

When someone has lived in stress, chaos, survival mode, or emotional instability for a long time, peace can initially feel uncomfortable.

Not because peace is wrong, but because the nervous system becomes conditioned to what is familiar.

Some people become so used to unpredictability that calmness feels suspicious.
They become so accustomed to emotional highs and lows that stability feels boring.
They become so familiar with chaos that healthy environments feel unfamiliar.

Healing changes this slowly.

Over time, you begin realizing that peace is not emptiness.
Peace is safety.

It is waking up without constant anxiety in your chest.
It is no longer needing to chase validation to feel worthy.
It is creating routines that support your well-being instead of sabotaging it.
It is surrounding yourself with people who do not make you question your value or emotional safety.

At first, peaceful living may feel quieter than what you are used to.

There may be moments when your mind wants to return to old patterns simply because they feel familiar. The human mind often confuses familiarity with security, even when what is familiar is harmful.

Choosing Yourself, One Day At a Time

This is why healing requires awareness.

You begin noticing when you are tempted to recreate old emotional environments.
You begin recognizing when restlessness is actually discomfort with calmness.
You begin understanding that your nervous system is learning a new way of existing.

Be patient with yourself through this process.

A peaceful life is not built overnight.
It is built through boundaries, healing, intentional choices, and repeatedly choosing environments that nourish rather than deplete you.

And perhaps one of the most beautiful parts of growth is this:
eventually, peace stops feeling unfamiliar.

Eventually, it begins feeling like home.

For today, remember this:
You are allowed to build a life that feels calm, safe, and emotionally steady.

Your Future Still Needs You

There will be moments in life when discouragement tries to convince you that it is too late.

Too late to change.
Too late to heal.
Too late to rebuild.
Too late to dream again.
Too late to become who you hoped you would be.

But the truth is, your future is still being written.

As long as you are here, there is still room for growth.
Still room for healing.
Still room for purpose.
Still room for transformation.

Many people quietly give up on themselves long before life asks them to. They stop believing things can improve, so they stop trying. They settle into survival and convince themselves that their best days are already behind them.

But your life is not over simply because you have struggled.

Your story is not ruined because you made mistakes.
Your future is not disqualified because of your past.

Some of the most compassionate, wise, grounded people become that way precisely because they walked through difficult seasons and chose to keep growing anyway.

Your experiences can become part of your strength instead of permanent proof of your defeat.

Choosing Yourself, One Day At a Time

There are still conversations you have not had.
Places you have not seen.
People you have not impacted.
Versions of yourself you have not yet met.

There are still dreams waiting for your courage.
Still opportunities waiting for your consistency.
Still healing waiting for your willingness.

And perhaps most importantly, there is still a future version of you hoping you do not give up too soon.

One healthy decision today may seem small, but it can completely alter the direction of your life over time.

Do not underestimate the power of continuing.

For today, remember this:
Your future still needs the version of you that refuses to give up.

The Life You Build Should Feel Like Yours

It is possible to spend years building a life that looks successful from the outside while internally feeling disconnected from it.

Meeting expectations.
Following timelines.
Chasing approval.
Trying to become who others expected you to be.

And somewhere along the way, many people lose touch with themselves.

They wake up one day realizing they have spent more time trying to fit into other people's ideas of success than asking themselves what truly brings them peace, meaning, and fulfillment.

But your life is not meant to be a performance for other people.

The life you build should feel like it belongs to you.

Your goals.
Your values.
Your pace.
Your priorities.
Your version of peace.

Not everyone will understand the choices that are healthiest for you. Some people may question your boundaries, your lifestyle, your healing, your dreams, or the direction your life is taking simply because it differs from what they would choose for themselves.

That does not mean you are wrong.

Choosing Yourself, One Day At a Time

A meaningful life is not created by constantly betraying yourself to meet external expectations.

It is created through alignment.

Alignment between:

- your values and your actions,
- your healing and your decisions,
- your goals and your priorities,
- your spirit and the life you are creating.

As you grow, you may begin wanting different things than you once did.
Quieter things.
Healthier things.
More intentional things.

You may care less about impressing people and more about feeling emotionally at peace when you wake up each day.

That is not settling.
That is maturity.

There is freedom in no longer needing your life to make sense to everyone else.

You only need the courage to stop abandoning yourself in order to fit into lives that were never fully yours to begin with.

For today, remember this:
The life you are building should nourish your spirit, not just impress other people.

Keep Becoming

There is no final moment where a person suddenly arrives fully healed, fully wise, fully confident, or fully complete.

Life is a continual process of becoming.

Becoming more honest.
More grounded.
More compassionate.
More aware.
More intentional.
More connected to yourself and the life you truly want to live.

Some seasons will stretch you.
Some seasons will humble you.
Some seasons will ask you to rest, rebuild, or begin again.

And through all of it, you are still becoming.

Do not let temporary setbacks convince you that growth is no longer happening. Some of the deepest transformation occurs quietly beneath the surface long before it becomes visible to anyone else.

There will be moments when you outgrow old versions of yourself.
Moments when your priorities change.
Moments when your definition of success evolves.
Moments when you realize that peace matters more than performance, and authenticity matters more than approval.

Allow yourself to evolve.

You are not meant to remain the same person forever.

Choosing Yourself, One Day At a Time

The person you were five years ago helped you survive.
The person you are becoming now is trying to help you truly live.

That requires courage.

Courage to heal differently.
Courage to choose differently.
Courage to stop repeating patterns that no longer align with your future.
Courage to believe that your life can continue becoming more meaningful, more peaceful, and more aligned over time.

There is beauty in realizing that growth is not something you finish.
It is something you practice.

One decision at a time.
One boundary at a time.
One prayer at a time.
One day at a time.

And perhaps that is what choosing yourself really means:
continuing to return to your own life with presence, honesty, and willingness no matter how many times you must begin again.

For today, remember this:
You are not finished becoming who you are meant to be.

You Do Not Need to Rush Your Healing

In a world that moves quickly, many people begin treating healing like something they should be able to complete on a deadline.

They want to "be over it" already.
Over the heartbreak.
Over the grief.
Over the anxiety.
Over the shame.
Over the past.

So when healing takes longer than expected, frustration begins to replace compassion.

But healing is not a race.

Some experiences change people deeply. Some losses take time to process. Some wounds require gentleness, patience, and repeated care before they begin to soften.

You are not weak because certain things still affect you.

There are parts of healing that cannot be forced.

The heart heals differently than a checklist.
The nervous system heals differently than a calendar.
The soul heals differently than productivity culture would like people to believe.

There may be days when you feel strong and grounded, followed by days when old emotions unexpectedly resurface. That does not mean you are failing. It means you are human.

Growth is rarely linear.

Choosing Yourself, One Day At a Time

Sometimes healing happens in layers.
You revisit old pain with new wisdom.
You see old memories through a healthier lens.
You recognize patterns you once could not see.

This is part of becoming more aware, not proof that you are broken.

Be careful not to shame yourself for still healing from things that genuinely impacted your life.

You deserve patience too.

The same compassion you offer others during difficult seasons should also be extended inward.

There is no prize for pretending you are unaffected.
No reward for rushing yourself past emotions that still need care and understanding.

And perhaps one of the most healing realizations is this:
you do not need to become emotionally numb in order to become emotionally healthy.

For today, remember this:
You are allowed to heal at a pace that honors your humanity.

Your Boundaries Are an Act of Self-Respect

For many people, setting boundaries feels uncomfortable at first.

Especially if they were taught to prioritize everyone else's comfort above their own well-being.

They fear disappointing people.
Being misunderstood.
Being seen as selfish.
Losing connection.

So they say yes when they mean no.
They overextend themselves.
They tolerate behavior that drains them.
And slowly, resentment and exhaustion begin replacing peace.

But boundaries are not punishment.
They are protection.

Healthy boundaries help preserve your emotional, mental, physical, and spiritual well-being. They create space for healthier relationships, clearer communication, and a more grounded relationship with yourself.

A boundary is simply an honest acknowledgment of what you need in order to remain healthy and aligned.

It may sound like:

- "I cannot take that on right now."
- "I need rest."
- "That behavior is not okay with me."

Choosing Yourself, One Day At a Time

- "I need space."
- "I am no longer willing to participate in dynamics that harm my peace."

Not everyone will understand your boundaries, especially people who benefited from your lack of them.

That can be difficult.

But protecting your peace does not make you cruel.
Choosing yourself does not make you selfish.
Learning your limits does not make you difficult.

You are allowed to stop overexplaining your needs in order to make other people more comfortable with them.

Boundaries are not walls meant to isolate you from love and connection. They are healthy structures that allow relationships to exist without requiring self-abandonment.

And often, the more you heal, the more clearly you begin recognizing what drains you, what dishonors you, and what no longer aligns with the life you are trying to build.

There is wisdom in no longer giving unlimited access to people, environments, or behaviors that repeatedly disturb your peace.

Your energy matters.
Your time matters.
Your well-being matters.

For today, remember this:
Every healthy boundary you set is a reflection of growing self-respect.

You Are Allowed to Want a Softer Life

Not every meaningful life has to be loud, rushed, or constantly exhausting.

Some people spend years chasing achievement while secretly longing for something much simpler:
peace,
stability,
rest,
connection,
health,
purpose,
and room to breathe.

There is nothing wrong with wanting a softer life.

A life where your nervous system is not constantly overwhelmed.
A life where you are not always surviving the next emergency.
A life where home feels safe.
Where relationships feel mutual.
Where your days contain moments of stillness instead of constant pressure.

The world often glorifies burnout while quietly ignoring its cost.

People are praised for how much they can endure, how much they can sacrifice, and how much they can carry without collapsing. But surviving exhaustion is not the same thing as living well.

A softer life does not mean a lazy life.

It means becoming more intentional about what you allow into your mind, body, schedule, and spirit.

Choosing Yourself, One Day At a Time

It means choosing:

- healthier rhythms,
- healthier environments,
- healthier relationships,
- and healthier priorities.

It means understanding that peace is not something you stumble into accidentally. It is something you begin protecting through daily choices.

You may notice yourself wanting less chaos as you heal.
Less proving.
Less rushing.
Less drama.
Less noise.

That is not weakness.
That is wisdom.

As people grow emotionally, many begin realizing that fulfillment often lives in ordinary moments:
morning coffee in silence,
a walk outside,
a meaningful conversation,
a safe home

is not about avoiding responsibility.
It is about no longer abandoning yourself in the process of carrying it.

For today, remember this:
You are allowed to create a life that feels peaceful, grounded, and emotionally sustainable.

You Can Miss Someone and Still Choose Yourself

Healing sometimes requires accepting two truths at once.

You can love someone and still recognize that the relationship was unhealthy for you.
You can miss someone and still choose not to return.
You can cherish memories while understanding that certain connections no longer align with the life you are trying to build.

This is one of the hardest parts of growth.

People often believe that if they still feel sadness, longing, or attachment, it means they should go backward. But emotions are not always instructions. Sometimes they are simply reminders that something mattered deeply to you.

Missing someone does not automatically mean they belong in your future.

The heart takes time to adjust after emotional attachment, especially when a relationship carried hope, comfort, intensity, familiarity, or dreams about what life could have been.

Be gentle with yourself through that process.

There may be days when memories return unexpectedly.
Days when loneliness tries to romanticize what hurt you.
Days when you wonder if walking away was truly the right decision.

Choosing Yourself, One Day At a Time

In those moments, it is important to remember why you chose yourself in the first place.

Not every connection is meant to last forever.
Some relationships enter our lives to teach us,
to wake us up,
to mirror wounds,
to help us grow,
or to show us what we are no longer willing to tolerate.

That does not make the connection meaningless.
And it does not make you weak for still feeling emotions around it.

Healing is not about pretending you never cared.
It is about learning how to care about yourself too.

Sometimes choosing yourself means accepting that love alone is not always enough to sustain a healthy relationship.

Peace matters.
Consistency matters.
Safety matters.
Mutual effort matters.
Emotional health matters.

And perhaps one of the deepest forms of self-respect is refusing to return to places that repeatedly required you to abandon your own well-being.

For today, remember this:
You can miss someone and still choose the life that is healthiest for you.

Small Acts of Discipline Become Self-Love

People often think of self-love as a feeling.

But many of the deepest forms of self-love are actually choices.

Choosing to take care of your body even when motivation is low.
Choosing to save money for your future.
Choosing to attend the appointment.
Choosing to study after a long day.
Choosing to rest instead of self-destruct.
Choosing to tell yourself the truth.
Choosing to stop abandoning your own needs.

These moments may not always feel glamorous, but they quietly shape your life.

Discipline is often misunderstood as punishment.
In reality, healthy discipline can become one of the most compassionate things you give yourself.

Because discipline says:
"My future matters."
"My health matters."
"My peace matters."
"My goals matter."
"I matter."

The version of you that wants healing, stability, growth, and freedom is built through repeated acts of care, even on days when you do not immediately see results.

Choosing Yourself, One Day At a Time

A walk may not change your life overnight.
One healthy meal may not change your body overnight.
One study session may not earn the degree overnight.
One boundary may not heal everything overnight.

But consistency changes people.

Over time, small choices accumulate into confidence because you begin proving to yourself that you are capable of showing up for your own life.

And perhaps that is one of the most healing experiences of all:
becoming someone who no longer constantly abandons themselves when things feel difficult.

There is a quiet kind of self-respect that develops when your actions begin aligning with the future you say you want.

Not perfection.
Alignment.

You do not need to become obsessive or rigid to change your life. You simply need enough willingness to keep returning to the habits that nourish your well-being.

Every healthy decision is a vote for the person you are becoming.

For today, remember this:
Small acts of discipline are often small acts of self-love in disguise.

You Are Allowed to Protect Your Energy

Not every conversation deserves your explanation.
Not every opinion deserves your attention.
Not every invitation deserves your yes.

As you heal, you may begin noticing how deeply certain environments, relationships, and interactions affect your energy.

Some spaces leave you feeling inspired and grounded. Others leave you emotionally drained, anxious, overstimulated, or disconnected from yourself.

Pay attention to that.

Your energy is not unlimited.

And yet many people spend years giving emotional access to individuals and situations that repeatedly disturb their peace. They tolerate constant negativity, criticism, chaos, gossip, manipulation, or emotional inconsistency because they fear seeming selfish if they pull away.

But protecting your energy is not selfish.
It is responsible.

You cannot continue pouring from an exhausted spirit and expect to remain emotionally healthy.

Sometimes protecting your energy looks like:

- saying no without guilt,
- limiting certain interactions,
- taking breaks from social media,
- choosing rest,

- spending more time alone,
- declining drama,
- or becoming more intentional about who has access to your inner world.

Not everyone needs full access to you.

Some people only know how to connect through chaos.
Some people project their pain onto others.
Some people become uncomfortable when you begin growing beyond old dynamics.

You do not have to absorb everything around you in order to prove you are kind.

Compassion and boundaries can coexist.

In fact, protecting your peace often allows you to show up more fully and lovingly in the places that truly matter.

You deserve relationships and environments that feel emotionally safe, reciprocal, and nourishing — not constantly depleting.

And the more connected you become to yourself, the more naturally you will begin protecting the parts of your life that support your healing.

For today, remember this:
You are allowed to protect your peace without apologizing for it.

Becoming Takes Patience

There is a version of you you have not fully met yet.

A calmer version.
A wiser version.
A healthier version.
A more grounded and emotionally free version.

But becoming that person takes time.

Many people become discouraged because they expect transformation to happen quickly. They want immediate results, immediate healing, immediate clarity, immediate confidence. And when growth unfolds more slowly than expected, they begin doubting themselves.

But lasting transformation is rarely rushed.

A tree does not become deeply rooted overnight.
A healthy relationship is not built overnight.
A stable life is not built overnight.
A healed nervous system is not restored overnight.

The most meaningful things often require patience.

There will be seasons where progress feels obvious and exciting.
And there will be seasons where growth feels almost invisible.

Do not underestimate the invisible seasons.

So much of becoming happens quietly:
through repetition,
through consistency,
through reflection,
through ordinary choices made over long periods of time.

Choosing Yourself, One Day At a Time

You may not always notice your own growth while it is happening. But one day you may respond differently to something that once would have shattered you, and suddenly realize how much has changed within you.

That is growth.

Healing is not about becoming a completely different human being. It is about becoming more connected to your healthiest, most honest self.

And that process cannot be forced.

Be patient with the parts of you still learning.
Be patient with the parts of you still healing.
Be patient with the parts of you still finding their footing.

You are not late because growth takes time.
You are not failing because becoming feels gradual.

Some of the strongest people are built slowly and intentionally over years of choosing not to give up on themselves.

For today, remember this:
The person you are becoming is worth the patience the journey requires.

Your Worth Is Not Measured by Your Productivity

You live in a world that constantly encourages you to produce more, achieve more, accomplish more, and prove more.

And after a while, it becomes easy to confuse productivity with worth.

People begin believing they are only valuable when they are:
working,
helping,
performing,
achieving,
fixing,
or constantly staying busy.

So when they rest, slow down, struggle emotionally, or simply exist without producing something measurable, guilt begins to appear.

But your humanity is not something you have to earn.

Your worth does not disappear on the days you are tired.
Your value does not decrease because you need rest.
Your existence is not meaningful only when you are being useful to other people.

You are a human being, not a machine.

There is nothing wrong with ambition.
Nothing wrong with goals.
Nothing wrong with wanting to grow and contribute to the world.

Choosing Yourself, One Day At a Time

But when achievement becomes the only place you seek identity, exhaustion eventually follows.

A healthy life requires balance.

You deserve moments where you are allowed to simply:
breathe,
laugh,
heal,
connect,
create,
rest,
and exist without feeling pressured to constantly prove yourself.

Sometimes the most important thing you can do is pause long enough to reconnect with who you are underneath your responsibilities and roles.

Because you are more than:
your job title,
your accomplishments,
your income,
your appearance,
your grades,
or the expectations placed upon you.

Those things may describe parts of your life, but they do not define your inherent worth.

But real self-worth is deeper than performance.

It remains present even in seasons of rest, uncertainty, rebuilding, or transition.

For today, remember this:
You are worthy even on the days when you are simply trying your best to be human.

You Can Create a Different Future

Your past may explain parts of you, but it does not have to define the rest of your life.

Many people become trapped inside stories they no longer realize they are repeating:
"This is just who I am."
"My life will always be this way."
"People like me never really change."
"It's too late for me."

But healing begins when you stop treating your past as a permanent identity.

You are not limited to repeating every pattern you inherited, every coping mechanism you learned, or every belief that once developed while you were simply trying to survive.

A different future is created through awareness and choice.

Choice by choice.
Habit by habit.
Boundary by boundary.
Decision by decision.

You may not be able to rewrite everything that happened before this moment, but you can begin influencing what happens next.

That is powerful.

Every healthy choice matters:

- the choice to stay sober,
- the choice to ask for help,

- the choice to save money,
- the choice to return to school,
- the choice to heal instead of numb,
- the choice to walk away from what harms you,
- the choice to believe your future can still improve.

People often underestimate how dramatically a life can change over a few years of intentional living.

Not perfect living.
Intentional living.

A healthier future rarely appears all at once. It is built slowly through repeated decisions that align with the life you truly want to create.

And perhaps one of the most beautiful parts of growth is realizing that your future does not have to mirror your past in order for your story to make sense.

You are allowed to become someone different than who life once conditioned you to be.

You are allowed to heal beyond survival mode.

You are allowed to create a life rooted in peace, honesty, purpose, and self-respect.

For today, remember this:
The choices you make now have the power to shape a very different future.

There Is Strength in Starting Over

Starting over can feel humbling.

There are moments when rebuilding your life asks you to return to the beginning:
learning again,
healing again,
trusting again,
trying again.

And sometimes the ego resists this because it wants certainty, mastery, and immediate progress. It wants to skip the vulnerable parts of becoming.

But there is strength in allowing yourself to begin again anyway.

Strength in admitting:
"This version of my life no longer works."
"I want something healthier."
"I want more peace."
"I want to become someone different than who I have been."

Many people remain stuck not because change is impossible, but because they are too ashamed to start over.

They fear what others will think.
They fear appearing behind.
They fear failure more than remaining unhappy.

But every meaningful transformation requires humility.

No one builds a healthier life without first acknowledging what needs to change.

Choosing Yourself, One Day At a Time

Starting over may mean:
returning to school,
getting sober,
rebuilding finances,
leaving unhealthy relationships,
healing your body,
changing careers,
creating boundaries,
or simply learning how to care for yourself in ways you never were taught before.

None of that is failure.

It is courage.

And while starting over can initially feel uncomfortable, there is also something deeply hopeful about it.
Because beginning again means you still believe your future is worth investing in.

It means you have not completely given up on yourself.

Some of the most beautiful lives are built after people finally stop pretending they are fine and begin rebuilding honestly.

Not perfectly.
Honestly.

The beginning stages may feel slow and uncertain.
That is okay.

Every strong foundation once looked unfinished.

For today, remember this:
There is nothing shameful about starting over when your soul is asking for a different life.

You Are Allowed to Become More Intentional

There comes a point in healing where you stop wanting to live on autopilot.

You begin paying closer attention to:
how you spend your time,
what you consume,
who you surround yourself with,
how you speak to yourself,
what habits nourish you,
and what patterns quietly drain your peace.

You start realizing that a meaningful life is not built accidentally.

It is built intentionally.

Intentional living does not require perfection. It simply means becoming more aware of the choices shaping your life.

Instead of constantly reacting to everything around you, you begin asking:
"Does this align with the person I want to become?"
"Does this support my peace?"
"Does this help me grow?"
"Does this nourish my future or sabotage it?"

These questions slowly change the direction of your life.

Choosing Yourself, One Day At a Time

You may begin becoming more intentional with:
your finances,
your health,
your relationships,
your goals,
your energy,
and your healing.

At first, these changes may seem small or insignificant. But intentional choices accumulate over time.

A healthier meal.
An earlier bedtime.
A savings deposit.
A therapy appointment.
A walk outside.
A difficult but honest conversation.
A decision to stop returning to what continuously hurts you.

These moments matter more than people realize.

And perhaps one of the most beautiful parts of intentional living is that it slowly reconnects you to yourself.

You stop drifting through your days disconnected from your own needs and values.

You begin participating in your own life more consciously.

That awareness creates freedom.

For today, remember this:
A more peaceful life is often built through small intentional choices repeated over time.

Your Sensitivity Is Not a Weakness

Sensitive people often grow up believing there is something wrong with the way they experience the world.

They feel deeply.
Notice subtle shifts in energy.
Carry empathy for others.
Absorb tension in rooms.
Remember words long after they were spoken.

And because the world often praises emotional detachment more than emotional depth, sensitive people sometimes begin trying to harden themselves just to survive.

But sensitivity is not weakness.

Sensitivity is awareness.

The ability to feel deeply can become a beautiful strength when it is paired with healthy boundaries, self-awareness, and emotional regulation.

Sensitive people often:
love deeply,
care deeply,
create deeply,
and connect deeply.

They notice what others overlook.
They often become the encouragers, listeners, healers, creators, and protectors because they understand what it feels like to need compassion themselves.

Choosing Yourself, One Day At a Time

The problem is not sensitivity itself.
The problem is when sensitive people remain in environments that constantly overwhelm, invalidate, or emotionally exhaust them.

Without boundaries, sensitivity can turn into chronic depletion.

This is why healing matters.

As you grow, you learn:
how to protect your energy,
how to stop overabsorbing,
how to separate your emotions from everyone else's,
and how to care deeply without carrying the entire emotional weight of the world.

You do not need to become emotionally numb in order to become emotionally healthy.

You simply need balance.

Your sensitivity may actually be part of what makes you capable of creating meaningful connection, purposeful work, compassionate leadership, and authentic healing in both your own life and the lives of others.

Do not shame yourself for feeling deeply in a world that often teaches people to disconnect from themselves.

There is strength in emotional depth when it is rooted in self-awareness rather than self-abandonment.

For today, remember this:
Your sensitivity can become a gift when you learn how to care for yourself too.

The Right Life Will Not Require You to Betray Your Peace

There are opportunities, relationships, environments, and versions of success that may look impressive from the outside but quietly cost you your peace.

At first, you may try to convince yourself the sacrifice is worth it.

You tolerate constant stress.
Ignore exhaustion.
Accept emotional inconsistency.
Override your intuition.
Push past your limits.

And eventually, you realize you are building a life that no longer feels healthy to live inside.

This is why peace matters.

Not shallow comfort.
Not avoidance of responsibility.
But deep inner steadiness.

The kind of peace that allows you to breathe fully in your own life.

As you heal, your definition of success may begin changing. You may stop asking:
"How impressive does this look?"
and begin asking:
"How does this feel in my body, mind, and spirit?"

That shift changes everything.

Choosing Yourself, One Day At a Time

You begin valuing:
consistency over intensity,
alignment over appearance,
depth over performance,
and emotional safety over external validation.

The right life for you will not constantly require self-betrayal.

It will not demand that you abandon your health, your boundaries, your values, or your emotional well-being just to maintain it.

There may still be stress.
Responsibility.
Hard work.
Growth.
Challenge.

But healthy challenge is different from chronic inner turmoil.

Pay attention to what your life feels like internally, not just how it appears externally.

Sometimes choosing peace means:
walking away,
slowing down,
starting over,
setting boundaries,
changing priorities,
or no longer chasing things that drain more from you than they truly give back.

For today, remember this:
The life meant for you should support your peace, not constantly destroy it.

You Are Allowed to Change Your Mind

Growth changes people.

As you heal, learn, and become more aware of yourself, your priorities may shift. The things you once wanted may no longer fit. The paths you once imagined may no longer feel aligned with the person you are becoming.

And sometimes that can feel uncomfortable because people often expect consistency from you even when your inner world has changed.

But you are allowed to evolve.

You are allowed to change your mind about:
what success means,
what relationships you want,
where you want to live,
how you want to spend your time,
what kind of life feels healthy,
and who you are becoming.

Changing your mind is not always instability.
Sometimes it is self-awareness.

Sometimes growth reveals truths you could not fully see before.

A person who is committed to healing and self-reflection will naturally outgrow certain ideas, habits, environments, and identities over time.

That is part of becoming more aligned.

The danger comes when people remain trapped inside old decisions simply because they fear disappointing others or appearing inconsistent.

Choosing Yourself, One Day At a Time

But forcing yourself to remain loyal to a version of your life that no longer fits your spirit creates quiet suffering.

You do not owe permanence to choices that are no longer healthy for you.

There is wisdom in reevaluating your direction as you gain new understanding about yourself and your needs.

You are not failing because your dreams changed.
You are not weak because your priorities shifted.
You are not dishonest because your heart wants something different now than it once did.

The healthiest people are often the ones willing to adapt honestly instead of pretending they have not changed.

Life is not about rigidly clinging to every old version of yourself.
It is about growing into deeper authenticity over time.

For today, remember this:
You are allowed to evolve into someone who wants different things than you once did.

You Do Not Need Everyone to Understand Your Journey

One of the hardest parts of personal growth is accepting that not everyone will understand the path you are taking.

Some people will question your decisions.
Some will minimize your dreams.
Some will project their fears onto your future.
Some simply will not see the vision that feels clear inside your heart.

That can feel lonely at times.

Especially when you are building something meaningful quietly and intentionally.

But not everyone is meant to understand every part of your journey.

People interpret life through the lens of their own experiences, limitations, fears, and beliefs. What feels expansive and aligned to you may feel unnecessary, unrealistic, or uncomfortable to someone else.

That does not mean you are wrong.

There is a difference between receiving wise counsel and seeking universal approval.

Wise counsel helps you grow.
Universal approval keeps you stuck trying to manage everyone else's perception of your life.

You will exhaust yourself if you constantly need other people to validate every decision before allowing yourself to move forward.

Choosing Yourself, One Day At a Time

Some dreams must first be protected privately while they are still becoming.

Some goals grow best in silence.
Some healing happens quietly.
Some transformations are meant to be lived before they are explained.

The people who are truly aligned with your growth will not require you to shrink your vision in order to make them comfortable.

And often, the results will eventually speak louder than the explanations ever could.

You do not need to argue with everyone who doubts you.
You do not need to convince everyone to believe in your future.

Your responsibility is not to manage everyone's opinion.
Your responsibility is to remain honest about the life you are trying to build.

Keep becoming.
Keep healing.
Keep choosing yourself.
Keep moving toward what feels aligned and meaningful to your spirit.

The right people will recognize the authenticity in your journey even if they do not fully understand every step of it.

For today, remember this:
You do not need universal understanding in order to continue growing into the life meant for you.

Your Healing Will Influence Other People

Sometimes people underestimate how deeply their own healing impacts the world around them.

They think healing is only personal.
Private.
Self-contained.

But healed people change environments.

A person who learns emotional regulation creates calmer relationships.
A person who learns self-respect models healthier boundaries.
A person who heals from shame often becomes safer for others to be authentic around.
A person who chooses growth instead of bitterness changes the emotional atmosphere they carry into families, workplaces, friendships, and communities.

Healing is contagious in ways people rarely talk about.

So is unhealed pain.

That is why your work matters.

Every time you choose:
honesty over avoidance,
peace over chaos,
growth over self-destruction,
compassion over cruelty,
or accountability over denial,
you influence more than just yourself.

You create ripple effects.

Choosing Yourself, One Day At a Time

Sometimes those ripple effects are visible.
Other times they are quiet and impossible to fully measure.

A kind conversation changes someone's day.
A compassionate leader changes a workplace culture.
A healed parent changes generations.
A person who shares their story honestly reminds others they are not alone.

Never underestimate the impact of becoming healthier.

The world does not only need more successful people.
It needs more emotionally healthy people.
More grounded people.
More self-aware people.
More compassionate people.

And perhaps one of the most meaningful things about healing is that it often transforms your presence before it transforms your circumstances.

People feel safer around someone who has done inner work.
More seen.
More understood.
Less judged.

Because healed people no longer need to project unresolved pain onto everyone around them.

Your healing matters not only because of what it does for you, but because of the kind of energy, leadership, love, and presence you bring into the lives of others as a result.

For today, remember this:
The work you do to heal yourself can quietly help heal the world around you too.

Some Days the Win Is Simply Not Giving Up

Not every day will feel inspiring.

Some days you will feel motivated, hopeful, and deeply connected to your future.

Other days may feel heavy.

Days where your energy is low.
Your emotions feel tangled.
Your progress feels invisible.
Your confidence feels quieter than usual.

On those days, it is important to remember that growth is not measured only by how productive, energized, or emotionally strong you feel.

Sometimes the victory is much simpler than that.

Sometimes the victory is:
getting out of bed,
showing up,
taking the walk,
going to work,
making the appointment,
staying sober,
studying anyway,
or choosing not to give up on yourself even when life feels difficult.

People often overlook the courage it takes to continue during emotionally exhausting seasons because persistence rarely looks glamorous from the outside.

But continuing matters.

Choosing Yourself, One Day At a Time

Especially on the days when you feel tempted to return to old patterns, isolate yourself completely, or believe the lie that your effort no longer matters.

It matters.

Not every season of life is meant for massive visible progress. Some seasons are about endurance. Some are about staying committed to yourself while quietly moving through difficult emotions, uncertainty, grief, stress, or transition.

There is strength in continuing gently.

You do not always need to conquer the entire mountain in one day. Sometimes you simply need to keep placing one foot in front of the other.

Small movement still counts.
Quiet resilience still counts.
Resting without quitting still counts.

Be careful not to shame yourself for being human during difficult seasons.

Even slow days are part of the journey.

For today, remember this:
Some days, the bravest thing you can do is simply refuse to give up on yourself.

The Way You Care for Yourself Becomes Your Foundation

A healthy life is not built only through major accomplishments.

It is built through the daily ways you care for yourself.

The food you eat.
The sleep you get.
The thoughts you repeat.
The people you allow close to you.
The boundaries you maintain.
The habits you practice consistently over time.

These ordinary choices quietly become the foundation beneath your future.

Many people try to build meaningful lives while neglecting the very things that sustain them. They push through exhaustion, ignore emotional pain, silence their needs, and continue operating as though their well-being is optional.

But eventually, the body keeps score.
The mind keeps score.
The nervous system keeps score.

And what is neglected internally eventually begins affecting everything externally.

Self-care is often misunderstood as indulgence.
In reality, healthy self-care is maintenance.

It is learning how to create a life your body, mind, and spirit can sustainably live inside.

This does not require perfection.
It requires awareness and consistency.

Choosing Yourself, One Day At a Time

Some days self-care may look restorative:
rest,
stillness,
quiet,
or solitude.

Other days it may look disciplined:
exercise,
healthy eating,
financial responsibility,
hard conversations,
therapy,
or choosing growth over temporary comfort.

Not all care feels comforting in the moment.

Sometimes caring for yourself means making decisions your future self will thank you for later.

Healing often begins when you stop treating yourself like an afterthought.

When you begin recognizing that your energy, health, emotions, and peace are not inconveniences to ignore, but important parts of your humanity that deserve attention.

The life you want to build requires a healthy foundation beneath it.

And that foundation is strengthened one intentional choice at a time.

For today, remember this:
The way you care for yourself today is shaping the life you will be able to sustain tomorrow.

You Deserve Relationships That Feel Safe

Not just exciting.
Not just intense.
Not just familiar.

Safe.

Emotionally safe.
Mentally safe.
Spiritually safe.

Relationships should not constantly leave you anxious, confused, emotionally depleted, or questioning your worth.

Love is not supposed to feel like walking on eggshells all the time.

Healthy connection creates room for honesty, vulnerability, growth, and peace. It allows you to be human without fear that your emotions, needs, or boundaries will automatically become reasons for rejection.

Safety in relationships does not mean there will never be conflict.
Healthy relationships still require communication, accountability, and effort.

But there is a difference between normal human difficulty and environments that repeatedly damage your nervous system.

Pay attention to how people make you feel consistently.

Choosing Yourself, One Day At a Time

Do you feel calmer around them or constantly on edge?
Do you feel respected or emotionally dismissed?
Do you feel supported in your growth or subtly discouraged from evolving?
Do you feel emotionally safe enough to be authentic?

These things matter.

Many people stay in emotionally unhealthy dynamics because chaos feels familiar. They mistake intensity for love because their nervous system became conditioned to inconsistency.

Healing changes this slowly.

As you grow, you begin valuing:
consistency over confusion,
peace over drama,
depth over performance,
and emotional safety over temporary validation.

You stop romanticizing relationships that continuously destabilize you.

And perhaps one of the most healing realizations is understanding that you do not need to earn basic emotional respect.

You deserve relationships where:
communication feels honest,
care feels mutual,
boundaries are respected,
and your nervous system is not constantly forced into survival mode.

For today, remember this:
You deserve relationships that allow your heart to feel safe, respected, and at peace.

Your Story Is Still Unfolding

It is easy to believe that the chapter you are in right now will last forever.

When life feels heavy, uncertain, lonely, exhausting, or unclear, the mind often struggles to imagine anything different. Pain has a way of narrowing perspective until all you can see is the difficulty directly in front of you.

But your story is still unfolding.

This moment is not the entire story.
This setback is not the entire story.
This season is not the entire story.

There are still parts of your life you have not lived yet.

There are still experiences waiting to shape you,
relationships waiting to find you,
opportunities waiting to meet you,
and versions of yourself waiting to emerge through the choices you continue making today.

One of the most important things you can remember during difficult seasons is this:
life changes.

People heal.
Circumstances shift.
New doors open.
Perspectives evolve.
Pain softens.
Strength grows quietly over time.

The version of you reading this now is already different from versions of yourself that once believed they would never survive certain things.

Choosing Yourself, One Day At a Time

Growth often happens so gradually that you do not fully recognize it until you pause and look back.

There may still be uncertainty ahead.
There may still be healing left to do.
There may still be dreams that require patience and persistence.

But uncertainty does not mean hopelessness.

Your future has not been canceled simply because the current chapter feels difficult.

Keep investing in yourself.
Keep choosing healing.
Keep building slowly.
Keep showing up for your life even when progress feels quiet.

The life you are creating may still be taking shape beneath the surface in ways you cannot fully see yet.

Some chapters are meant for planting roots before the visible growth appears.

For today, remember this:
Your current season is only one chapter, not the conclusion of your story.

You Are Allowed to Take Up Space

Many people spend years making themselves smaller.

Smaller in conversations.
Smaller in relationships.
Smaller in dreams.
Smaller in needs.
Smaller in personality.

They learn to quiet themselves in order to avoid rejection, conflict, criticism, or disappointment from others.

Over time, this self-minimizing becomes so automatic that they no longer realize how much of themselves they have hidden away just to feel accepted.

But healing slowly teaches you something important: you were never meant to disappear inside your own life.

You are allowed to have needs.
You are allowed to have opinions.
You are allowed to have dreams that matter to you.
You are allowed to speak honestly, set boundaries, ask questions, and exist fully without apologizing for your humanity.

Taking up space does not mean becoming arrogant or self-centered.

It means no longer believing that your worth depends on how invisible, agreeable, or emotionally convenient you can make yourself for everyone else.

There is a difference between kindness and self-erasure.

Choosing Yourself, One Day At a Time

You can be compassionate without abandoning yourself.
You can be humble without shrinking your voice.
You can care deeply about others while still acknowledging that your own life matters too.

The world benefits when people become more authentic, not more hidden.

Your ideas matter.
Your creativity matters.
Your perspective matters.
Your presence matters.

And perhaps one of the most healing experiences is realizing that the right people will not require you to become less of yourself in order to belong.

Healthy connection allows room for your full humanity.

You deserve spaces where you do not constantly feel pressured to perform, hide, or minimize who you are.

You deserve to exist fully within your own life.

For today, remember this:
You are allowed to take up space in the world without apologizing for your existence.

Your Life Does Not Need to Look Like Everyone Else's

There is so much pressure in the world to follow a certain script.

Go here.
Achieve this by this age.
Build life in this order.
Measure success this way.
Want what everyone else wants.

And if your life begins unfolding differently, it can sometimes make you question yourself.

But a meaningful life is not created through imitation.

Your journey may not look conventional.
Your timeline may not look traditional.
Your dreams may not look identical to the people around you.

That does not make your life less valuable.

Some people are meant to live loudly.
Others quietly.
Some are builders.
Some are healers.
Some are creators.
Some are caretakers.
Some reinvent themselves multiple times throughout life.

There is no single correct way to exist.

The danger comes when people betray themselves trying to fit inside lives that were never truly aligned with their spirit in the first place.

Choosing Yourself, One Day At a Time

Healing often requires releasing comparison.

Comparison steals peace because it encourages you to measure your inner life against someone else's external appearance. But you never fully know what another person is carrying internally.

A life that looks impressive from a distance may feel emotionally empty up close.

What matters most is not whether your life mirrors someone else's path.
What matters is whether your life feels honest to you.

Does it support your well-being?
Does it align with your values?
Does it allow room for authenticity, peace, growth, and purpose?

Those questions matter more than social expectations ever will.

You do not need to force yourself into someone else's version of success in order for your life to be meaningful.

There is freedom in allowing your journey to unfold in its own unique way.

For today, remember this:
Your life does not have to look like anyone else's in order to be beautiful and worthwhile.

Healing Sometimes Means Grieving the Version of You That Had to Survive

There are versions of yourself that existed only because life required survival.

The version that stayed quiet to avoid conflict.
The version that accepted less than they deserved because loneliness felt frightening.
The version that numbed emotions because feeling everything at once was too overwhelming.
The version that kept functioning even while internally exhausted.

Those versions of you were not weak.

They were trying to protect you with the tools they had at the time.

And yet, as healing begins, there can also be grief.

Grief for the years spent disconnected from yourself.
Grief for opportunities missed while surviving.
Grief for the ways you abandoned your own needs trying to make it through difficult seasons.

This grief is normal.

Healing is not only about celebrating growth.
Sometimes it is also about mourning what you endured before you knew healthier ways to live.

Be gentle with yourself in this process.

You do not need to hate old versions of yourself in order to grow beyond them.

In fact, part of healing is learning compassion for the person you once were.

Choosing Yourself, One Day At a Time

The person who made mistakes.
The person who stayed too long.
The person who was afraid.
The person who was overwhelmed.
The person who coped imperfectly.

That person still deserved love, understanding, and care.

Many people try to shame themselves into transformation, but shame rarely creates sustainable healing. Compassion creates safety, and safety allows growth to happen more honestly.

You can acknowledge unhealthy patterns without condemning yourself entirely.

You can recognize that certain coping mechanisms no longer serve your future while still understanding why they developed in the first place.

Your past self was doing the best they could with the awareness, pain, and resources they had at the time.

Now you know more.
Now you are healing differently.
Now you are becoming someone new.

For today, remember this:
You do not need to hate who you once were in order to honor who you are becoming.

You Are Allowed to Build Slowly

Not every meaningful life is built quickly.

Some dreams take years.
Some healing takes years.
Some foundations need time to strengthen before the next chapter can fully support the weight of what you are trying to create.

And yet, many people feel ashamed when their progress looks slower than expected.

They compare timelines.
Question themselves.
Rush decisions.
Push beyond healthy limits trying to "catch up."

But slow does not mean stagnant.

There is wisdom in building carefully.
Wisdom in creating stability before expansion.
Wisdom in allowing your life to develop in ways that are sustainable instead of rushed.

A slowly built life often carries deeper roots.

When you build slowly, you learn:
patience,
discipline,
consistency,
self-awareness,
and how to stay committed even when immediate results are not visible.

You begin valuing long-term peace over short-term appearances.

Choosing Yourself, One Day At a Time

The world may celebrate rapid success stories, but many of the healthiest lives are built quietly over time through ordinary, repeated acts of intention.

A savings account built deposit by deposit.
A degree earned class by class.
A healthier body built walk by walk.
A peaceful mind built boundary by boundary.
A healed life built choice by choice.

Do not underestimate gradual transformation.

You are not failing because your growth looks steady instead of dramatic.
You are not behind because you are taking your time to build wisely.

Some people rush into futures they are emotionally, financially, or spiritually unprepared to sustain.

You are allowed to build differently.

To pace yourself.
To protect your peace.
To prioritize sustainability over appearance.

A strong life is not measured by how quickly it was built, but by how deeply it can support the person living inside it.

For today, remember this:
There is strength and wisdom in building your life slowly and intentionally.

Your Future Is Built by the Choices You Repeat

Every life is shaped by repetition.

The thoughts you repeat.
The habits you repeat.
The boundaries you repeat.
The excuses you repeat.
The healing practices you repeat.
The ways you speak to yourself each day.

Over time, repeated choices become patterns.
Patterns become identity.
And identity quietly shapes the direction of your future.

This is why small daily decisions matter so much.

A single healthy choice may feel insignificant in the moment, but repeated over months and years, it becomes transformation.

One walk becomes a healthier body.
One class becomes a degree.
One savings deposit becomes stability.
One boundary becomes peace.
One honest conversation becomes healing.
One day of sobriety becomes a completely different life.

People often underestimate consistency because consistency feels ordinary while it is happening.

It is not dramatic.
It is not flashy.
It is simply repeated commitment.

But repeated commitment changes people.

The same is true in the opposite direction.
Repeated self-neglect, avoidance, dishonesty, or self-abandonment also shape a person over time.

This is why awareness matters.

Your future is not determined only by major life events.
It is heavily influenced by the small choices you continue practicing when no one is watching.

And perhaps one of the most empowering realizations is this:
you do not need to transform your entire life overnight.

You simply need to begin choosing differently more consistently.

Healing is rarely one giant decision.
It is many small decisions repeated long enough to create a new way of living.

There will be setbacks.
Days where you lose momentum.
Moments where old habits try to pull you backward.

That does not erase your progress.

You can always begin choosing again.

For today, remember this:
The future you desire is being shaped by the choices you consistently repeat today.

You Are Not Too Much for the Right People

Many people learn to suppress parts of themselves after experiencing rejection, misunderstanding, or emotional inconsistency.

They become quieter.
More guarded.
More careful about expressing emotions, needs, dreams, or vulnerability.

Eventually they begin wondering:
“Am I too sensitive?”
“Too emotional?”
“Too ambitious?”
“Too deep?”
“Too much?”

But often, the problem was never your humanity.

The problem was being in spaces where your humanity was not handled with care.

The right people will not make you feel burdensome for having emotions.
They will not punish you for communicating honestly.
They will not require you to constantly minimize yourself in order to maintain connection.

Healthy relationships create room for authenticity.

That does not mean every person will fully understand you, agree with you, or connect with you deeply. Not every connection is meant to be lifelong or intimate.

But the people who are aligned with your life will not consistently make you feel like you must earn the right to exist fully as yourself.

Choosing Yourself, One Day At a Time

You deserve relationships where:
your sensitivity is respected,
your growth is supported,
your boundaries are honored,
and your presence feels welcomed rather than tolerated.

Healing often involves unlearning the belief that you must constantly shrink yourself to remain lovable.

You are allowed to have depth.
You are allowed to care deeply.
You are allowed to want meaningful connection.
You are allowed to speak honestly about your needs and emotions.

The goal is not to become less human in order to avoid rejection.
The goal is to become more authentic while learning discernment about who truly deserves access to your inner world.

Not everyone will be able to meet you at your depth.
That is okay.

Do not mistake incompatibility for personal unworthiness.

For today, remember this:
You are not too much for people who genuinely value and respect your heart.

A Peaceful Life Is Created Through Repeated Honest Choices

Peace rarely arrives all at once.

It is built slowly through the decisions you make every day.

The decision to stop lying to yourself about what hurts.
The decision to leave environments that continually drain you.
The decision to care for your health instead of neglecting it.
The decision to set boundaries instead of silently building resentment.
The decision to choose long-term healing over temporary escape.

These choices may feel small individually, but together they begin changing the emotional atmosphere of your life.

Many people search for peace while continuing patterns that constantly disturb it.

They ignore their intuition.
Avoid difficult conversations.
Stay connected to what repeatedly wounds them.
Abandon their own needs trying to keep everyone else comfortable.

And then they wonder why peace feels so distant.

But peace is not something you stumble into accidentally.

Peace is something you protect.

It requires honesty.

Choosing Yourself, One Day At a Time

Honesty about:
what no longer aligns,
what needs healing,
what drains your energy,
what you truly want,
and what your spirit can no longer continue carrying.

Honesty can feel uncomfortable at first because it often asks you to confront truths you once avoided in order to survive.

But avoiding truth does not create peace.
It creates internal conflict.

Healing begins when your outer life slowly starts becoming more aligned with your inner truth.

When your actions begin matching your values.
When your boundaries begin matching your needs.
When your habits begin supporting your future instead of sabotaging it.

That alignment creates steadiness.

And over time, a steadier life creates a steadier nervous system.

A peaceful life is not necessarily a perfect life.
It is a life where you no longer constantly betray yourself in order to maintain it.

For today, remember this:
Peace is often built through repeated honest choices that honor your well-being.

The Person You Are Becoming Deserves Your Patience

Growth can feel frustrating when you can clearly see the life you want but have not fully arrived there yet.

You may know the kind of person you are trying to become:
healthier,
more disciplined,
more peaceful,
more financially stable,
more emotionally grounded,
more connected to your purpose.

And yet there are still days where old habits appear.
Old fears surface.
Old emotions return.
Old insecurities speak loudly.

That can make you feel discouraged.

But becoming someone new is not an instant event.
It is a relationship you build with yourself over time.

The version of you that you are growing into deserves patience while learning how to exist differently.

There are patterns within you that were built over years.
Ways of thinking shaped by survival.
Habits created during pain, stress, loneliness, or uncertainty.

Healing those patterns takes repetition and grace.

You do not become healthier by hating yourself every time you struggle.

Choosing Yourself, One Day At a Time

You become healthier by continuing to return to yourself with honesty and compassion instead of giving up entirely.

Think about how gently you would encourage someone you love who was trying to rebuild their life. You would likely recognize their effort even before the final results appeared.

You deserve that same compassion from yourself.

Your growth does not need to happen perfectly in order to be real.

There will be days where you feel strong and aligned. There will also be days where you feel tired, emotional, uncertain, or discouraged.

Neither type of day defines your entire journey.

Transformation is rarely measured by one isolated moment. It is measured by your willingness to continue returning to the life you are trying to build.

And perhaps one of the kindest things you can remember is this:
the person you are becoming is learning through every step of the process, including the imperfect ones.

For today, remember this:
Your future self deserves the patience and compassion required to keep growing into them.

You Are Allowed to Protect the Life You Are Building

As you begin healing and growing, you may notice something changing within you.

You become more selective.

More selective with your time.
Your energy.
Your relationships.
Your habits.
Your environment.
Your focus.

Not because you suddenly think you are better than others, but because you finally understand how easily peace can be disrupted when you stop protecting what matters.

A healthier life requires maintenance.

Just as a garden cannot thrive when constantly neglected or trampled, your emotional well-being also requires care and protection.

This means there may be moments when you:
decline invitations,
limit certain conversations,
step away from unhealthy dynamics,
say no without overexplaining,
or spend more time nurturing your future than entertaining distractions.

That is not selfishness.
That is stewardship.

You are protecting the life you are trying to create.

Choosing Yourself, One Day At a Time

Not every opportunity deserves access to your attention.
Not every relationship deserves unlimited emotional access.
Not every habit deserves to come with you into the next chapter of your life.

As you grow, you may become less interested in chaos and more interested in consistency.
Less interested in proving yourself and more interested in preserving your peace.
Less interested in external validation and more interested in internal alignment.

This shift is healthy.

People who are deeply committed to growth eventually realize that protecting their well-being is part of maintaining the future they want.

Because one of the hardest truths about healing is this: it is possible to work very hard to build a healthier life while still allowing certain people, patterns, or environments to repeatedly destabilize it.

Protection matters.

Not fear-based isolation.
Not emotional walls.
But wise discernment.

You deserve a life that feels emotionally sustainable.
And that requires becoming intentional about what you allow to repeatedly enter your mind, body, and spirit.

For today, remember this:
You are allowed to protect the peace, healing, and future you are working so hard to build.

Halfway to Becoming

There will come a day when you look back at the version of yourself who first began this journey and realize just how much has changed.

Not only externally, but internally.

The way you think.
The way you love.
The way you speak to yourself.
The way you handle pain.
The way you protect your peace.
The way you show up for your own life.

Transformation often happens so gradually that you do not notice it while it is unfolding.

You simply keep making choices.
Keep healing.
Keep rebuilding.
Keep returning to yourself one day at a time.

And then suddenly, one ordinary moment reveals how different you have become.

You respond calmly where you once reacted impulsively.
You rest without guilt.
You walk away from what once would have kept you trapped.
You begin trusting yourself more.
You stop abandoning your needs to keep everyone else comfortable.

These quiet changes matter.

Choosing Yourself, One Day At a Time

Healing is not always loud.
Sometimes it looks like becoming softer with yourself.
More honest.
More intentional.
More emotionally safe to live inside your own mind and body.

There is something sacred about reaching the middle of a journey and realizing:
"I did not give up."

Not because every day was easy.
Not because you always felt strong.
But because some deeper part of you kept believing your life was worth fighting for.

That matters more than perfection ever will.

And while there is still more growth ahead, do not rush past the progress already made.

Pause long enough to honor:
the courage it took to begin,
the honesty it took to change,
and the resilience it took to continue through difficult seasons.

You are not the same person who started this journey.

And that is something worth acknowledging.

For today, remember this:
Healing happens one choice at a time, and every step forward matters.

Your Presence Matters More Than Perfection

Many people spend their lives chasing perfection because they believe perfection will finally make them worthy of love, success, acceptance, or peace.

So they keep trying to say the right thing,
look the right way,
achieve enough,
fix enough,
prove enough.

And yet perfection remains unreachable because human beings were never meant to live without flaws, emotions, mistakes, or vulnerability.

What people often need most is not perfection.
It is presence.

Presence in conversations.
Presence in relationships.
Presence in parenting.
Presence in leadership.
Presence in friendship.
Presence in your own life.

A present person listens.
A present person notices.
A present person makes others feel seen and valued.

And perhaps one of the most healing things you can learn is that your value does not come from performing flawlessly. Your value often comes from the energy, honesty, and humanity you bring into the spaces you enter.

People rarely remember perfection as deeply as they remember presence.

Choosing Yourself, One Day At a Time

They remember:
who made them feel safe,
who truly listened,
who showed up consistently,
who treated them with kindness,
who stayed genuine in a world that often encourages performance instead of authenticity.

This applies to yourself too.

You do not need to become perfect before you allow yourself to participate fully in your life.

You are allowed to:
learn while imperfect,
grow while imperfect,
love while imperfect,
heal while imperfect,
and begin again while imperfect.

Perfectionism often delays healing because it convinces people they must “arrive” before they are worthy of peace.

But healing is not about becoming flawless.
It is about becoming more honest, compassionate, grounded, and connected to yourself over time.

Your humanity is not a problem to solve.

It is something to honor with care and presence.

For today, remember this:
Your authentic presence will always matter more than trying to appear perfect.

You Can Build a Life That Feels Safe to Stay In

Many people spend years trying to escape their own lives.

Escaping through distraction.
Overworking.
Numbing.
Constant busyness.
Unhealthy relationships.
Self-destructive habits.
Fantasy about becoming someone else somewhere else.

But healing slowly shifts this desire.

Instead of constantly searching for escape, you begin wanting to create a life that actually feels safe, peaceful, and sustainable to live inside.

A life you no longer need to run from.

This changes the kinds of questions you ask yourself.

Instead of:
"How do I impress people?"
you begin asking:
"How do I create peace?"

Instead of:
"How do I keep proving my worth?"
you begin asking:
"How do I care for my well-being?"

Instead of:
"How do I survive this?"
you begin asking:
"How do I build something healthier long term?"

Choosing Yourself, One Day At a Time

These are powerful shifts.

Because a meaningful life is not built only through external accomplishments. It is built through emotional sustainability.

Can your nervous system rest in the life you are creating?
Can your spirit breathe there?

These things matter.

You deserve:
a home that feels peaceful,
relationships that feel emotionally safe,
work that aligns with your values,
routines that support your health,
and habits that nourish rather than destroy you.

As you heal, your standards may begin changing.
You may become less interested in intensity and more interested in steadiness.
Less interested in chaos and more interested in calm.
Less interested in appearances and more interested in alignment.

That is growth.

A healthy life is not necessarily the loudest or most impressive life.
Often, it is simply a life where your mind, body, and spirit no longer feel trapped in constant survival mode.

You are allowed to build it too.

For today, remember this:
You deserve a life that feels emotionally safe to remain fully present inside.

The Way Forward Is Built Through Daily Courage

People often imagine courage as something dramatic.

A huge leap.
A fearless moment.
A life-changing decision made without hesitation.

But most courage is much quieter than that.

Courage is often found in ordinary moments.

Getting back up after disappointment.
Having the difficult conversation.
Attending the appointment.
Applying for the opportunity.
Setting the boundary.
Asking for help.
Choosing sobriety again today.
Continuing to believe your life can improve even after painful seasons.

These moments may not look extraordinary from the outside, but they shape the direction of your future.

The truth is, courage rarely feels comfortable while it is happening.

Often, courage feels shaky.
Uncertain.
Vulnerable.

It feels like moving forward while still carrying fear.

Many people wait to feel completely confident before they act. But confidence is usually built through action, not before it.

Choosing Yourself, One Day At a Time

You become stronger by continuing.
You become wiser by learning through experience.
You become more grounded by repeatedly choosing growth over avoidance.

Healing requires daily courage because growth asks you to release familiar patterns while stepping into unfamiliar ways of living.

That can feel uncomfortable at first.

But discomfort is not always a sign you are moving in the wrong direction.
Sometimes it is simply evidence that you are expanding beyond old limitations.

You do not need to transform your entire life in one giant moment.
You only need enough courage to keep taking the next honest step.

One healthy choice.
One brave conversation.
One intentional day at a time.

And over time, those ordinary acts of courage become a completely different life.

For today, remember this:
Your future is built through the quiet courage you practice each day.

You Are Allowed to Feel Proud of the Life You Are Building

There is a difference between arrogance and quiet pride.

Arrogance seeks superiority.
Quiet pride recognizes growth.

Many people struggle to acknowledge their own progress because they fear appearing boastful. So they minimize their accomplishments, dismiss their resilience, and overlook how much effort it took simply to become who they are today.

But there is nothing wrong with honoring your growth.

You are allowed to feel proud of:
the healing you fought for,
the discipline you practiced,
the boundaries you learned,
the habits you changed,
the courage it took to begin again,
and the life you are slowly building through intentional choices.

Pride becomes unhealthy when it disconnects people from humility and compassion.
But healthy pride creates gratitude.

It allows you to pause and recognize:
"I have survived things that once felt impossible."
"I have grown."
"I am becoming someone different than I used to be."

That awareness matters.

Especially for people who spent years believing they were never enough.

Choosing Yourself, One Day At a Time

Healing often includes learning how to acknowledge your own progress without immediately criticizing yourself for not being farther ahead.

You do not need to diminish your growth in order to remain grounded.

You can remain humble while still recognizing your effort.
You can remain compassionate while still celebrating your healing.
You can remain teachable while still appreciating how far you have already come.

A healthy life is not built through constant self-rejection.

It is built through accountability balanced with compassion and self-respect.

And perhaps one of the most healing things you can learn is how to stand in gratitude for your progress while still remaining open to continued growth.

You are allowed to appreciate your becoming.

For today, remember this:
There is nothing wrong with quietly honoring the life you are working hard to build.

You Do Not Need to Carry Shame Forever

Shame has a way of convincing people that their mistakes, failures, struggles, or past choices permanently define who they are.

It whispers:
"You should have known better."
"You ruined everything."
"You'll never fully recover from this."
"You are unworthy because of what happened."

And over time, people begin carrying shame like a permanent identity instead of recognizing it as an emotional wound that also needs healing.

But you were never meant to live your entire life imprisoned by your past.

There is a difference between accountability and shame.

Accountability says:
"I made mistakes, and I want to grow."

Shame says:
"I am the mistake."

One leads to healing.
The other leads to self-destruction.

Many people made decisions while hurting, overwhelmed, lonely, addicted, afraid, emotionally immature, or simply trying to survive with the awareness they had at the time.

That does not erase consequences.
But it does mean your humanity deserves compassion too.

You are allowed to learn.
Allowed to evolve.
Allowed to become healthier than the version of yourself who once made painful choices.

The goal of healing is not pretending the past never happened.
The goal is no longer allowing the past to completely control how you see yourself.

Your mistakes may be part of your story, but they are not the entirety of your identity.

Some of the most compassionate, grounded people become that way because they walked through difficult seasons and chose to grow instead of remaining trapped in shame forever.

You are not beyond redemption because you struggled.
You are not disqualified from peace because you once lost your way.
You are not unworthy of a meaningful future because you are still healing from your past.

Healing asks you to stop carrying old shame as proof that you deserve suffering forever.

You deserve the opportunity to become someone new.

For today, remember this:
You do not have to spend the rest of your life punishing yourself for who you were while trying to survive.

Your Life Can Become More Peaceful Than It Once Was

There may have been a time when you believed stress, chaos, instability, or emotional exhaustion would always define your life.

Perhaps survival became so familiar that peace felt unrealistic.
Maybe you became used to carrying tension in your body, overthinking constantly, or waiting for the next difficult thing to happen.

But healing slowly teaches you that life does not always have to feel that heavy.

A more peaceful life is possible.

Not a perfect life.
Not a life without grief, responsibility, or challenge.

But a life where your nervous system no longer lives in constant survival mode.

Peace often begins with small changes:
getting enough rest,
creating healthier routines,
setting boundaries,
reducing chaos,
healing emotionally,
surrounding yourself with safer people,
making intentional decisions,
and learning how to stop abandoning yourself emotionally.

At first, peace may feel unfamiliar.

Choosing Yourself, One Day At a Time

You may even feel restless inside calm moments because your mind became conditioned to intensity. This is common for people who spent years living under chronic stress.

Be patient with yourself through that adjustment.

Your mind and body are learning a new way to exist.

And over time, something beautiful begins happening: you stop craving emotional chaos simply because it once felt familiar.

You begin preferring steadiness.
Honesty.
Rest.
Safety.
Consistency.
Alignment.

The things that once seemed boring may eventually become sacred to you because they allow your spirit to finally breathe.

A peaceful life is not built through one giant breakthrough.
It is built through repeated choices that honor your well-being.

Choice by choice.
Boundary by boundary.
Habit by habit.

For today, remember this:
You are allowed to create a life that feels calmer, healthier, and more emotionally safe than your past.

You Are Becoming the Person You Once Needed

There are moments in healing when you begin realizing that the care, understanding, encouragement, and safety you longed for in earlier seasons are slowly being created within yourself.

You begin speaking to yourself more gently.
Protecting your peace more intentionally.
Making healthier decisions.
Creating safer relationships.
Showing up for yourself in ways you once wished others would have.

That is powerful.

Because many people spend years searching externally for someone to rescue them while neglecting the relationship they have with themselves.

But healing changes this.

You begin becoming:
the encouragement,
the protection,
the stability,
the honesty,
and the compassion you once desperately needed.

This does not mean you no longer need connection or support from others. Human beings still need love, community, and care.

But there is something deeply healing about no longer completely abandoning yourself while waiting for someone else to save you.

You become more dependable to your own spirit.

Choosing Yourself, One Day At a Time

You begin noticing:
"I handled that differently."
"I protected my peace."
"I chose growth."
"I stayed."
"I did not give up on myself this time."

These moments matter more than you realize.

Healing is not always dramatic.
Sometimes it simply looks like becoming emotionally safer for yourself to live with.

The younger version of you may have needed:
validation,
protection,
stability,
comfort,
or guidance they did not fully receive.

And now, through awareness and healing, you are slowly learning how to offer some of those things inwardly.

That is not selfish.
That is restoration.

And perhaps one of the most beautiful parts of growth is realizing that you are no longer entirely powerless inside your own life.

You are learning how to care for yourself differently.

For today, remember this:
Part of healing is becoming the kind of person your younger self would have felt safe with.

The Right Future Requires a Healthier You

Sometimes people become so focused on reaching the next goal that they forget to ask whether they are becoming healthy enough to truly sustain the future they desire.

A peaceful relationship requires emotional health.
Meaningful leadership requires self-awareness.
Long-term success requires balance.
A fulfilling life requires a foundation strong enough to support it.

This is why healing matters.

Not because you need to become perfect before good things happen, but because unresolved pain eventually influences every part of your life:
your relationships,
your habits,
your decisions,
your health,
your finances,
your boundaries,
and the way you respond to stress and uncertainty.

Growth is not only about achieving more.
It is also about becoming more capable of handling life in healthier ways.

You may want:
love,
success,
purpose,
stability,
peace,
or opportunity.

Choosing Yourself, One Day At a Time

But the healthiest version of those things often requires a healthier relationship with yourself first.

That process can feel slow at times.

Healing your nervous system.
Changing old patterns.
Learning emotional regulation.
Building discipline.
Creating healthier routines.
Practicing honesty.
Rebuilding self-trust.

These are not distractions from your future.
They are preparation for it.

A meaningful life is not sustained by external success alone.
It is sustained by inner steadiness.

And perhaps one of the wisest things you can do is stop rushing toward outcomes while neglecting the internal work required to hold them well.

The future you want deserves a version of you that is emotionally grounded enough to fully live inside it.

That takes patience.
Awareness.
Humility.
Consistency.

But the work matters.

For today, remember this:
The life you desire will be supported by the healing and growth you commit to now.

You Are Allowed to Want Peace More Than Approval

Many people spend years shaping their lives around other people's opinions.

Trying to be liked.
Trying to avoid criticism.
Trying to meet expectations.
Trying to keep everyone comfortable.

And in the process, they slowly lose connection with themselves.

Because constantly seeking approval often requires self-abandonment.

You stay quiet when you need honesty.
You say yes when your spirit needs rest.
You tolerate what hurts you to avoid disappointing others.
You keep performing versions of yourself that no longer feel authentic simply because they are familiar to everyone around you.

But healing changes your priorities.

At some point, peace becomes more valuable than approval.

Not because you stop caring about people.
But because you finally understand the emotional cost of constantly betraying yourself to maintain acceptance.

Choosing Yourself, One Day At a Time

You begin realizing:
not everyone will understand your boundaries,
your healing,
your goals,
your growth,
or the direction your life is taking.

And that is okay.

You are not responsible for managing every opinion people have about your life.

You are responsible for living honestly enough that your own spirit can breathe inside the life you are creating.

There is freedom in no longer needing universal validation before making healthy decisions for yourself.

You stop asking:
"Will everyone approve?"
and begin asking:
"Does this support my peace?"
"Does this align with who I am becoming?"
"Does this honor my well-being?"

Those questions create a more grounded life.

Approval is temporary.
Peace is sustaining.

And often, the people who truly love and respect you will eventually understand that your boundaries, healing, and growth are not acts of rejection toward them. They are acts of care toward yourself.

For today, remember this:
You are allowed to prioritize peace over constantly seeking approval from others.

Your Healing Is Allowed to Be Imperfect

There is a quiet pressure many people place on themselves once they begin healing.

They think:
“If I’m growing, I should not struggle anymore.”
“If I’m healing, I should always respond calmly.”
“If I’ve learned the lesson, I should never feel this emotion again.”

But healing does not erase your humanity.

You will still have hard days.
Still feel grief sometimes.
Still become tired, emotional, uncertain, or overwhelmed.
Still encounter moments where old fears, habits, or insecurities resurface.

That does not mean your growth disappeared.

It means you are human.

Healing is not measured by never struggling again.
It is measured by how you care for yourself when struggle appears.

Do you abandon yourself completely?
Or do you return to yourself with honesty and compassion?

That is the difference.

There may be moments when you:
need rest,
need support,
need to apologize,
need to reset,
need to begin again.

None of that erases the progress you have made.

People often imagine healed individuals as people who never feel pain anymore. But emotionally healthy people still feel deeply. The difference is they no longer allow pain to completely define their identity or control every decision they make.

They learn how to move through difficult emotions without becoming entirely consumed by them.

And perhaps one of the most freeing realizations is understanding that perfection was never the goal.

Presence.
Awareness.
Honesty.
Growth.
Compassion.
Alignment.

These things matter far more than flawless behavior ever will.

You do not need to become emotionally perfect to deserve peace, love, purpose, or healing.

You are already worthy while still becoming.

For today, remember this:
Your healing does not have to look perfect in order to be real and meaningful.

You Are Allowed to Trust the Pace of Your Life

It can be difficult to trust your own timing when the world constantly encourages urgency.

Faster success.
Faster healing.
Faster achievement.
Faster transformation.

People are taught to believe that if something meaningful is not happening quickly, they must be failing.

But not everything valuable grows rapidly.

Some things require seasons of preparation that are not immediately visible.

Healing takes time.
Wisdom takes time.
Stability takes time.
Self-trust takes time.
A deeply rooted life takes time.

And while it may feel frustrating at times, there is often purpose in slower seasons.

A slower pace can create space for:
reflection,
self-awareness,
intentional decisions,
healthier foundations,
and emotional maturity.

Many people rush toward futures they are not internally prepared to sustain.

But a life built slowly and intentionally often carries deeper peace because it was created with awareness instead of desperation.

Trusting your pace does not mean avoiding effort or responsibility.
It means understanding that your life does not need to unfold according to someone else's timeline in order to be meaningful.

There may be moments when you feel behind compared to others.
Moments when your progress feels quieter or less visible.

Do not let comparison pressure you into abandoning what is healthy for you.

You are allowed to:
take your time,
move thoughtfully,
heal gradually,
and build carefully.

Some dreams are meant to unfold over years because the person carrying them is also still becoming.

And perhaps one of the most healing realizations is understanding that you do not need to rush your becoming in order for it to matter.

Your life is not late simply because it is unfolding differently.

For today, remember this:
You are allowed to trust the pace at which your life and healing are unfolding.

You Deserve to Feel at Home Within Yourself

One of the deepest forms of healing is learning how to feel safe inside your own presence.

Not constantly fighting yourself.
Not constantly criticizing yourself.
Not constantly trying to escape yourself.

But learning how to exist within your own life with greater peace, compassion, and honesty.

Many people spend years disconnected from themselves.

They know how to perform.
How to survive.
How to stay busy.
How to meet expectations.

But they do not know how to simply be with themselves without judgment, anxiety, distraction, or self-rejection.

Healing slowly changes this relationship.

You begin listening to yourself more carefully.
Respecting your limits.
Paying attention to your emotions instead of automatically suppressing them.
Creating routines that support your well-being.
Choosing environments that feel safer to your nervous system.

And little by little, you stop feeling like a stranger to yourself.

This process takes time.

Choosing Yourself, One Day At a Time

Especially if you spent years abandoning your own needs in order to survive, please others, or maintain unhealthy environments.

Be patient with yourself as you learn how to reconnect inwardly.

You are not trying to become perfect.
You are learning how to become emotionally safer for yourself to live with.

That means:
speaking to yourself more gently,
setting healthier boundaries,
making choices aligned with your future,
allowing rest,
and no longer treating your humanity like a problem to fix.

There is something sacred about reaching a place where your mind, body, and spirit no longer feel constantly at war with each other.

Where peace begins feeling possible internally, not just externally.

You deserve that kind of relationship with yourself.

Because no matter where life takes you, you will always carry your own presence with you.

For today, remember this:
Healing is helping you create a home within yourself that feels safer, calmer, and more compassionate to live inside.

The Small Choices Are Changing You

People often underestimate the impact of small decisions because they focus only on dramatic transformation.

They expect life to change through one giant breakthrough, one perfect opportunity, or one extraordinary moment.

But most meaningful change happens much more quietly than that.

A life changes through repetition.

The walk you almost skipped.
The money you decided to save.
The boundary you finally honored.
The prayer you whispered in private.
The healthy meal.
The chapter you studied after a long day.
The moment you chose honesty instead of avoidance.

These things may seem small individually, but together they begin shaping a completely different future.

Every repeated choice strengthens something within you.

Repeated discipline strengthens self-trust.
Repeated honesty strengthens alignment.
Repeated healing strengthens emotional stability.
Repeated self-respect strengthens boundaries.
Repeated care strengthens peace.

This is why consistency matters more than intensity.

Intensity can create temporary motivation.
Consistency creates transformation.

Choosing Yourself, One Day At a Time

You do not need to overhaul your entire life overnight to become healthier. You simply need enough willingness to keep returning to the choices that support the person you are trying to become.

Some days those choices will feel easy.
Other days they will feel exhausting.

Keep choosing anyway.

The strongest foundations are often built through ordinary decisions repeated long enough to become part of who you are.

And perhaps one of the most beautiful things about growth is realizing that your future is not determined solely by your past. It is also shaped by the daily choices you continue making now.

Every healthy decision is quietly teaching your mind, body, and spirit:
"We are building something different."

For today, remember this:
The small choices you make consistently are slowly shaping the person and life you are becoming.

You Do Not Need to Fear Becoming Different

Growth changes people.

Not always dramatically at first, but gradually and deeply.

Your priorities shift.
Your habits evolve.
Your boundaries strengthen.
Your definition of peace changes.
The things you once tolerated no longer feel acceptable.
The things you once chased may no longer feel fulfilling.

And sometimes this can feel unsettling because change often creates distance between who you were and who you are becoming.

You may notice:
certain conversations no longer interest you,
certain environments exhaust you,
certain relationships feel misaligned,
or certain dreams begin transforming into something new.

This is a natural part of healing.

You are not meant to remain the exact same person forever.

The version of you that existed in earlier seasons was shaped by the awareness, wounds, coping mechanisms, and circumstances of that time.

But growth invites evolution.

Choosing Yourself, One Day At a Time

Not because your past self was unworthy, but because your future requires new levels of awareness and alignment.

Some people resist growth because they fear losing familiarity.
Others fear how people around them may react if they begin changing.

But becoming healthier will naturally shift parts of your life.

You may become calmer.
More intentional.
More selective.
More emotionally honest.
Less willing to tolerate chaos or self-abandonment.

That is not something to fear.

That is evidence that your healing is creating movement.

You are allowed to outgrow patterns that once felt normal.
You are allowed to desire healthier relationships, healthier routines, healthier goals, and a healthier internal life.

Transformation often feels uncomfortable before it feels natural because your nervous system is learning new ways of existing.

Be patient with yourself through that transition.

For today, remember this:
You are allowed to become different as you heal, grow, and move toward a healthier life.

A Gentle Life Is Still a Meaningful Life

Not every meaningful life needs to be loud, fast, or constantly impressive.

Some lives are built quietly.

Through kindness.
Through consistency.
Through healing.
Through presence.
Through small daily acts of care that may never receive public recognition but still deeply matter.

There is beauty in gentleness.

A gentle life may look like:
morning prayer,
a peaceful home,
healthy routines,
honest work,
meaningful conversations,
time in nature,
quiet growth,
steady healing,
and relationships that feel emotionally safe.

The world often glorifies intensity and constant achievement, but many people are secretly exhausted from trying to maintain lives that never allow them to rest.

You are allowed to desire something softer.

Not smaller.
Not less meaningful.
Simply more aligned with peace.

Gentleness is not weakness.

Choosing Yourself, One Day At a Time

It takes strength to choose:
calm over chaos,
rest over burnout,
healing over avoidance,
authenticity over performance,
and intentional living over constant urgency.

Some people mistake gentleness for lack of ambition because they have only learned to associate worth with pressure and exhaustion.

But a grounded, emotionally healthy life can still hold purpose, discipline, growth, leadership, and impact.

In fact, many people create their greatest influence not through force, but through the steady way they treat themselves and others over time.

A gentle life creates room for:
presence,
gratitude,
connection,
reflection,
and emotional sustainability.

You do not have to constantly push yourself to the edge in order for your life to matter.

You deserve moments where your spirit can breathe.

Moments where your nervous system can soften.
Moments where you no longer feel trapped in survival mode.

For today, remember this:
A peaceful and gentle life can still be a deeply purposeful and beautiful one.

You Are Allowed to Become More Protective of Your Peace

As you heal, you may notice yourself becoming less available for things that once felt normal.

Less available for chaos.
Less available for emotional games.
Less available for constant negativity.
Less available for relationships that repeatedly leave you feeling drained, anxious, or disconnected from yourself.

This shift is not coldness.
It is awareness.

Healing changes your tolerance for what disturbs your peace.

You begin understanding that your emotional energy is valuable. Your nervous system matters. Your mental and spiritual well-being deserve care and protection.

And once you truly recognize how hard you have worked to create more peace within yourself, you naturally become more intentional about what you allow to repeatedly disrupt it.

This may mean:
setting firmer boundaries,
limiting certain conversations,
protecting your time,
saying no more often,
or stepping away from people and environments that continuously create instability in your life.

Not everyone will understand these changes.

Choosing Yourself, One Day At a Time

Some people benefited from the version of you that overextended yourself, ignored your own needs, and remained endlessly available no matter how exhausted you became.

But you are allowed to evolve beyond self-abandonment.

Protecting your peace does not make you selfish.
It makes you responsible for your well-being.

A healthier life requires discernment.

Not everything deserves access to your inner world.
Not every invitation deserves your energy.
Not every opinion deserves emotional space inside your mind.

As you grow, you may find yourself craving:
more quiet,
more honesty,
more consistency,
more emotional safety,
and more intentional connection.

That is not weakness.
That is your spirit recognizing what it needs in order to remain healthy.

Peace is precious.
And the more healing you do, the more clearly you understand its value.

For today, remember this:
You are allowed to protect your peace with intention, wisdom, and self-respect.

The Life You Want Requires Consistency More Than Perfection

Many people delay change because they believe they need to do everything perfectly before their efforts truly count.

So if they miss a workout,
make a mistake,
have an emotional day,
lose momentum,
or fall into an old habit for a moment,
they immediately feel like they failed.

But perfection is not what changes lives.

Consistency does.

A healthy life is not built through flawless days.
It is built through repeated willingness to return to your goals, your healing, and your values even after imperfect moments.

The people who transform their lives are not usually the people who never struggle.
They are the people who keep coming back.

Back to the walk.
Back to the routine.
Back to the boundary.
Back to the healing work.
Back to themselves.

That matters.

One imperfect day does not erase your progress.
One setback does not cancel your future.
One difficult season does not define your entire journey.

Choosing Yourself, One Day At a Time

Growth requires flexibility and self-compassion because human beings are not machines.

There will be days when your energy is low.
Days when emotions feel heavier.
Days when life feels overwhelming.

You do not need to collapse your entire identity every time you experience a hard moment.

You can simply begin again.

Again and again if necessary.

The goal is not to become perfect.
The goal is to become more aligned over time.

More honest.
More intentional.
More self-aware.
More committed to your own well-being.

And perhaps one of the most healing realizations is understanding that lasting change is often less about intensity and more about your willingness to continue returning to the life you are trying to build.

Slow consistency creates strong foundations.

For today, remember this:
You do not need perfect days to create a meaningful and healthier life.

You Are Allowed to Believe in a Better Future for Yourself

Sometimes the hardest thing to rebuild after painful seasons is hope.

Not surface-level positivity.
Not pretending everything is fine.

Real hope.

The kind that quietly believes your life can still become healthier, calmer, more meaningful, and more aligned than it once was.

Pain can make people fearful of hope because disappointment teaches the heart to protect itself. After enough difficult experiences, some people stop allowing themselves to fully imagine better possibilities because they fear being hurt again.

But healing asks you to open your life to possibility once more.

Not recklessly.
Not naively.
But courageously.

You are allowed to believe:
that peace is possible,
that healthier relationships are possible,
that emotional stability is possible,
that meaningful work is possible,
that joy is possible,
that healing is possible,
and that your future does not have to mirror your hardest seasons forever.

Choosing Yourself, One Day At a Time

Believing in a better future does not mean ignoring reality.
It means refusing to let pain become the only thing shaping your vision of what your life can become.

Some of the most transformative moments begin quietly:
a decision to return to school,
a commitment to sobriety,
a healthier routine,
a boundary,
a prayer,
a savings goal,
a choice to stop abandoning yourself.

Small acts of hope change lives.

You do not need to have every answer right now.
You do not need to control every outcome.

You only need enough willingness to continue participating in your own becoming.

The future is shaped by what you repeatedly choose to nurture.

Nurture peace.
Nurture healing.
Nurture discipline.
Nurture honesty.
Nurture hope.

Your life is still unfolding.

For today, remember this:
You are allowed to believe that your future can become healthier and more beautiful than your past.

You Deserve to Experience Your Own Life Fully

Many people move through life disconnected from the present moment.

Always rushing.
Always worrying.
Always replaying the past or trying to control the future.

And in the process, they miss the life that is actually happening right in front of them.

Healing slowly teaches you how to return to the present.

To notice:
the morning light,
the feeling of fresh air,
the sound of laughter,
the comfort of stillness,
the taste of coffee,
the peace of a quiet walk,
the feeling of being fully alive inside an ordinary moment.

Presence matters.

Because life is not only found in major milestones.
It is also found in the quiet spaces between them.

Many people postpone living while waiting for everything to finally feel perfect:
"When I heal more."
"When I make more money."
"When I lose the weight."
"When life settles down."
"When I finally arrive somewhere."

But life is happening now.

Not every moment will feel beautiful.
Not every season will feel easy.

But your life still deserves your presence even while you are healing, rebuilding, and becoming.

You deserve to experience:
your relationships,
your body,
your dreams,
your surroundings,
your emotions,
your growth,
and your humanity with greater awareness instead of constantly moving through your days disconnected from yourself.

This does not require perfection.
It requires attention.

Attention to what nourishes your spirit.
Attention to what brings peace.
Attention to the moments that remind you that life is more than survival.

There is something deeply healing about learning how to fully arrive inside your own life again.

Not constantly escaping it.
Not constantly numbing it.
But participating in it with honesty and openness.

For today, remember this:
You deserve to be fully present for the life you are working so hard to build.

Your Life Does Not Have to Be Fueled by Fear Anymore

Fear can shape a person's life quietly over time.

Fear of rejection.
Fear of failure.
Fear of being alone.
Fear of disappointing others.
Fear of starting over.
Fear of not being enough.

And when fear becomes the primary force behind your decisions, it slowly pulls you away from yourself.

You say yes when you mean no.
Stay where you no longer feel healthy.
Hide parts of who you are.
Delay dreams that matter to you.
Keep choosing survival over growth because familiarity feels safer than change.

But healing begins changing your relationship with fear.

You realize that fear does not always mean stop.
Sometimes fear simply means you are standing at the edge of growth.

The goal is not to become fearless.
The goal is to stop allowing fear to completely control the direction of your life.

Courage and fear often exist together.

You can feel uncertain and still move forward.
You can feel vulnerable and still choose honesty.
You can feel afraid and still choose growth.

Choosing Yourself, One Day At a Time

Some of the most important decisions you will ever make may happen while your hands are shaking internally.

That is okay.

What matters is your willingness to continue choosing alignment over avoidance.

Fear often wants to keep life small because smallness feels predictable.
But your healing may require:
new boundaries,
new habits,
new environments,
new dreams,
or new ways of seeing yourself.

Growth asks you to trust that your future can hold more peace and possibility than your fear wants you to believe.

You are no longer required to organize your entire life around avoiding discomfort.

A meaningful life requires movement.
Honesty.
Risk.
Vulnerability.
Hope.

And perhaps one of the most powerful realizations is understanding that the life waiting for you on the other side of fear may feel far more aligned than the life built entirely around avoiding it.

For today, remember this:
You are allowed to build a life guided more by healing and purpose than by fear.

You Are Allowed to Become Someone New

There may be people who only know the older versions of you.

The version who stayed quiet.
The version who tolerated too much.
The version who lived in survival mode.
The version who doubted themselves constantly.
The version who carried shame, fear, or exhaustion everywhere they went.

And sometimes, when you begin changing, people may struggle to understand the person you are becoming.

That can feel uncomfortable.

Because growth often requires releasing identities that once felt familiar, even if they were rooted in pain.

You are allowed to outgrow old versions of yourself.

You are allowed to become:
healthier,
calmer,
more disciplined,
more honest,
more grounded,
more emotionally aware,
and more protective of your peace.

Transformation does not erase your past.
It simply means your past no longer gets to define the entirety of your future.

Some people may continue relating to you through outdated assumptions because they have not witnessed your internal healing fully.

That is okay.

You do not need everyone to fully understand your becoming in order for your growth to be real.

What matters is whether you are becoming more aligned with the life your spirit is asking you to create.

Healing often changes:
your priorities,
your boundaries,
your habits,
your relationships,
your routines,
your goals,
and even your sense of identity.

This can feel disorienting at times because growth asks you to let go of old narratives about who you are allowed to be.

But you are not trapped inside old versions of yourself forever.

You are allowed to evolve beyond survival.
Beyond shame.
Beyond self-abandonment.
Beyond the expectations that once kept you small.

A healthier future may require a different version of you than the one who first began the journey.

And that is not betrayal.
That is becoming.

For today, remember this:
You are allowed to grow beyond the versions of yourself that were created only to survive.

Healing Is Also Learning How to Receive

Many people know how to give.

They know how to help.
Support.
Encourage.
Show up for others.
Carry responsibility.
Take care of everyone else's needs.

But receiving can feel much harder.

Receiving support.
Receiving rest.
Receiving kindness.
Receiving love.
Receiving help without guilt.
Receiving care without feeling like they must immediately earn it back.

This often happens when people learned early in life that their value came primarily from what they could provide, fix, or carry for others.

So they become comfortable overextending themselves while feeling uncomfortable simply being cared for.

But healing asks you to learn balance.

You are not meant to exist only as someone who gives endlessly while silently depleting yourself.

You deserve support too.

Choosing Yourself, One Day At a Time

You deserve relationships where care flows both directions.
You deserve moments where you are allowed to exhale instead of constantly holding everything together.
You deserve spaces where you do not always have to be the strong one.

Receiving does not make you weak.
It makes you human.

In fact, allowing yourself to receive healthy support often requires vulnerability and trust.

It requires believing:
"I am still worthy even when I am not performing."
"I do not need to earn every act of care through exhaustion."
"I am allowed to have needs too."

This can feel deeply uncomfortable at first for people who became used to self-reliance as protection.

Be patient with yourself through that process.

Healing is not only about learning how to care for others better.
It is also about learning how to stop neglecting yourself in the process.

There is something deeply restorative about finally allowing yourself to experience support, rest, compassion, and care without immediately feeling guilty for needing them.

For today, remember this:
You are allowed to receive the same care, compassion, and support that you so freely offer to others.

You Are Not Wasting Your Life by Healing Slowly

Sometimes people become frustrated with themselves because healing takes longer than they expected.

They feel like they should already be farther along.
Already stronger.
Already "over it."
Already fully healed and thriving.

And when growth unfolds slowly, they begin believing they are wasting time.

But healing is not wasted time.

Learning how to care for yourself is not wasted time.
Rebuilding your peace is not wasted time.
Developing emotional awareness is not wasted time.
Creating healthier habits is not wasted time.

In fact, these things often become the foundation that makes the rest of your future possible.

Many people rush through life emotionally disconnected from themselves, chasing achievement while silently carrying unresolved pain into every area of their lives.

You are doing different work.

Inner work.

Choosing Yourself, One Day At a Time

The kind of work that changes:
how you love,
how you lead,
how you cope,
how you communicate,
how you handle stress,
how you treat yourself,
and how you show up in the world.

That work matters deeply, even when the results are not immediately visible.

There are seasons where external progress may appear slower because so much energy is being invested internally:
healing the nervous system,
changing patterns,
building discipline,
processing grief,
learning boundaries,
or reconnecting with yourself honestly.

These seasons are not meaningless detours.

They are preparation.

A healthier future often requires a healthier internal foundation beneath it.

And perhaps one of the most important things to remember is this:
you are not falling behind because you are taking the time to heal properly.

That is valuable work.

For today, remember this:
The time you spend healing and rebuilding yourself is not time wasted — it is time shaping your future.

You Can Create Stability Even If Life Once Felt Chaotic

Some people grow up or live through seasons where instability becomes normal.

Emotional unpredictability.
Financial stress.
Relationship chaos.
Constant anxiety.
Always waiting for the next problem to appear.

Over time, the nervous system adapts to survival mode. Chaos begins feeling familiar, even when it is exhausting.

But familiarity is not the same thing as health.

Healing teaches you that stability can be created intentionally.

Not instantly.
Not perfectly.
But gradually.

Through routines.
Boundaries.
Healthier habits.
Financial responsibility.
Emotional awareness.
Safer relationships.
Honest choices repeated consistently over time.

Stability is not built through one giant breakthrough.
It is built through many small moments of self-respect.

Choosing Yourself, One Day At a Time

Going to bed earlier.
Saving money.
Keeping promises to yourself.
Protecting your peace.
Attending the appointment.
Choosing consistency over emotional extremes.
Learning how to regulate instead of react.

These things matter.

At first, stability may even feel unfamiliar or uncomfortable if your body became conditioned to constant stress. Some people unconsciously seek chaos simply because calmness feels strange to them.

Be patient with yourself through that adjustment.

Your nervous system is learning a new experience: safety.

You are allowed to build:
a calmer home,
a healthier body,
steadier finances,
more peaceful relationships,
and a life that no longer constantly feels like emotional survival.

The process may feel slow.
That is okay.

Strong foundations are usually built gradually.

You are not doomed to repeat chaos forever.

For today, remember this:
Small intentional choices can slowly create the stability your heart and nervous system have been longing for.

Your Future Deserves the Healthiest Version of You

The future you dream about is not built only through ambition.

It is built through alignment.

Alignment between:
your goals and your habits,
your dreams and your discipline,
your healing and your choices,
your values and the life you create every day.

Many people want a healthier future while continuing patterns that quietly sabotage it.

They neglect rest.
Ignore emotional wounds.
Avoid difficult truths.
Abandon themselves repeatedly while trying to achieve external success.

But eventually, unresolved pain influences every area of life.

This is why healing matters so deeply.

Not because you need to become perfect before your future can begin, but because the healthiest version of your future requires a healthier relationship with yourself.

A peaceful relationship requires emotional maturity.
Long-term success requires balance.
Purposeful leadership requires self-awareness.
A meaningful life requires inner stability.

Choosing Yourself, One Day At a Time

The future you want deserves a version of you capable of sustaining it.

That means:
caring for your body,
protecting your peace,
creating healthy habits,
building emotional awareness,
practicing honesty,
learning boundaries,
and becoming intentional about the life you are creating.

This work may not always feel glamorous.
Often it feels quiet and repetitive.

But quiet consistency changes lives.

Every healthy decision strengthens your foundation.

Every moment you choose healing over avoidance strengthens your future.

And perhaps one of the most powerful things you can realize is this:
you are not only building external success.
You are building the internal capacity to actually enjoy and sustain the life you are creating.

That matters.

Because achievement without peace eventually feels empty.

For today, remember this:
The healthiest version of your future will be supported by the healing and choices you commit to today.

You Are Allowed to Rest Without Explaining Yourself

Many people feel the need to justify their exhaustion before allowing themselves to rest.

They believe they must reach a breaking point first.
Become completely overwhelmed first.
Finish every responsibility first.

So they keep pushing beyond their limits while quietly disconnecting from themselves.

But rest is not something you must earn through suffering.

You are allowed to rest because you are human.

You are allowed to slow down without presenting evidence that your exhaustion is "serious enough."
You are allowed to take care of your body before burnout forces you to.
You are allowed to create space for recovery even if the world around you continues moving quickly.

Rest is not laziness.
Rest is maintenance.

Your nervous system needs recovery.
Your body needs care.
Your mind needs stillness.
Your spirit needs room to breathe.

Without rest, even meaningful things begin to feel heavy.

Healing often includes learning how to stop treating yourself like a machine that exists only to perform, produce, and carry responsibility endlessly.

Choosing Yourself, One Day At a Time

You are more than your output.

And perhaps one of the most difficult parts of healing for some people is realizing that they were taught to feel guilty for having normal human needs.

Needs for:
sleep,
quiet,
solitude,
emotional support,
stillness,
or simply time to recover.

But your humanity is not an inconvenience.

There is wisdom in listening to yourself before exhaustion becomes collapse.

There is wisdom in recognizing that sustainable growth requires balance.

A healthier life is not built through constant depletion.
It is built through rhythms of effort and restoration working together.

You do not need permission to care for yourself.

For today, remember this:
You are allowed to rest without apologizing for being human.

Healing Changes What You Are Willing to Tolerate

As you grow, your standards begin changing.

Not only for other people, but for yourself.

Things that once felt normal may no longer feel healthy.
Conversations that once felt acceptable may now feel draining.
Environments that once felt familiar may now feel emotionally exhausting.

This can be surprising at first.

You may notice yourself pulling away from:
constant chaos,
one-sided relationships,
self-destructive habits,
unnecessary drama,
or situations that repeatedly disturb your peace.

That is not weakness.
That is awareness.

Healing changes your relationship with what you are willing to tolerate.

You begin realizing that protecting your peace matters more than preserving unhealthy patterns simply because they are familiar.

You start noticing:
how certain people affect your nervous system,
how certain habits affect your energy,
how certain environments affect your emotional well-being.

Choosing Yourself, One Day At a Time

And once awareness grows, it becomes harder to ignore what no longer aligns with the life you are trying to build.

This can feel lonely at times because growth often creates distance between you and old versions of yourself, old environments, or old dynamics.

But you are not required to remain loyal to things that continuously harm your well-being.

You are allowed to:
want healthier relationships,
create healthier routines,
choose calmer environments,
protect your energy,
and stop abandoning yourself in order to maintain connections that consistently cost you your peace.

Healing often looks like becoming more honest about what your spirit can no longer comfortably carry.

That honesty creates change.

And while change can initially feel uncomfortable, it also creates space for healthier experiences, healthier relationships, and a healthier relationship with yourself.

You are not becoming difficult.
You are becoming more aligned.

For today, remember this:
Growth often changes what your mind, body, and spirit are willing to tolerate.

Your Life Is Allowed to Feel Good to You

So many people build lives based on appearances.

What looks impressive.
What earns approval.
What seems successful from the outside.

But a life can look beautiful publicly while feeling emotionally exhausting privately.

Healing changes the questions you ask yourself.

Instead of:
"How does this appear?"
you begin asking:
"How does this feel?"

Does your life feel peaceful?
Does your body feel safe?
Does your spirit feel nourished?
Do your relationships feel reciprocal?
Does your work align with your values?
Do your routines support your well-being?

These questions matter deeply.

Because you are the one who has to live inside your life every day.

You deserve a life that feels good to your nervous system, not just one that looks impressive to other people.

Choosing Yourself, One Day At a Time

This may mean:
choosing peace over performance,
health over appearance,
balance over burnout,
or authenticity over approval.

As you heal, your definition of fulfillment may become quieter and more intentional.

You may crave:
restful mornings,
meaningful connection,
steady growth,
safe relationships,
creative expression,
emotional stability,
and a home that feels calm.

That is not settling.
That is alignment.

There is nothing shallow about wanting a life that supports your emotional, physical, and spiritual well-being.

A healthy life should not constantly require you to abandon yourself in order to maintain it.

And perhaps one of the most freeing realizations is understanding that you no longer need to organize your life around proving something to everyone else.

You are allowed to build a life that genuinely feels nourishing to you.

For today, remember this:
Your life is allowed to feel peaceful, meaningful, and emotionally sustainable to your own heart.

You Are Not Starting From Nothing

There may be moments when rebuilding your life makes you feel like you are starting over completely.

Like you lost time.
Lost direction.
Lost pieces of yourself along the way.

But you are not starting from nothing.

You are starting from experience.

Experience that taught you what no longer works.
Experience that deepened your empathy.
Experience that strengthened your awareness.
Experience that revealed what truly matters to you.

Painful seasons often leave people feeling behind, but many of those seasons also quietly build wisdom that cannot be learned through comfort alone.

You now know things you once did not know:
what drains you,
what heals you,
what peace feels like,
what boundaries matter,
what self-abandonment costs,
what kind of life your spirit no longer wants to live inside.

That awareness matters.

Even your mistakes hold lessons.
Even your setbacks contain information.
Even your difficult seasons helped shape the person you are becoming now.

Healing does not erase the past.
It transforms your relationship with it.

Choosing Yourself, One Day At a Time

You stop seeing yourself only through the lens of regret and begin recognizing that every chapter — even the painful ones — contributed to your growth, your resilience, and your understanding of yourself.

The version of you rebuilding now is not naive.
Not empty-handed.
Not without strength.

You carry:
hard-earned wisdom,
greater self-awareness,
deeper compassion,
and clearer vision than you once had.

That changes how you move forward.

You may still be rebuilding.
Still healing.
Still becoming.

But you are not beginning from nothing.

You are beginning from experience, awareness, and the decision to create something healthier than before.

For today, remember this:
You are not starting over empty-handed — you are starting again with wisdom you did not have before.

You Are Allowed to Want More Than Survival

For some people, survival became the primary focus for so long that they forgot life could be about anything more.

Just getting through the day.
Paying the bills.
Managing the stress.
Holding everything together.
Making it to tomorrow.

And when survival mode lasts long enough, people often stop asking themselves deeper questions about what they truly want from life.

But healing invites those questions back into the light.

What brings you peace?
What makes you feel alive?
What kind of life actually feels meaningful to you?
What would it look like to build a future rooted not only in survival, but in alignment, purpose, and emotional well-being?

You are allowed to want more than merely existing through your days exhausted and disconnected from yourself.

Choosing Yourself, One Day At a Time

You are allowed to want:
joy,
rest,
purpose,
health,
stability,
meaningful relationships,
creative fulfillment,
spiritual connection,
and a life that feels emotionally sustainable.

This does not make you selfish or unrealistic.

It makes you human.

Many people settle into chronic survival because it feels familiar, even when it hurts. They become so focused on managing immediate stress that they stop imagining what a healthier future could look like.

You deserve moments where you are fully present.
Moments where your nervous system can relax.
Moments where your spirit feels connected to something deeper than simply getting through another day.

That question changes everything.

Because a meaningful life is not built only through endurance.
It is also built through intention, healing, and allowing yourself to believe that peace and fulfillment are possible for you too.

For today, remember this:
You are allowed to create a life centered around more than just survival.

The Relationship You Have With Yourself Shapes Everything Else

No matter where you go, who you love, what you achieve, or how your circumstances change, you will still carry yourself into every part of your life.

Your thoughts.
Your habits.
Your beliefs.
Your wounds.
Your healing.
Your inner dialogue.

This is why the relationship you have with yourself matters so deeply.

If you constantly criticize yourself, abandon your needs, ignore your boundaries, or speak to yourself with contempt, that pain eventually influences every other area of your life.

But when you begin healing your relationship with yourself, everything else begins shifting too.

You make healthier decisions.
You recognize unhealthy dynamics more quickly.
You protect your peace more intentionally.
You stop chasing validation from people who cannot offer genuine connection.

Healing teaches you how to become emotionally safer for yourself.

How to listen inwardly.
How to care for your needs without shame.
How to stop treating your humanity like a burden.

Choosing Yourself, One Day At a Time

This does not mean becoming self-absorbed.
It means becoming self-aware.

There is a difference.

A healthy relationship with yourself creates:
better boundaries,
healthier relationships,
greater emotional stability,
stronger self-trust,
and deeper alignment with the life you are trying to build.

You begin realizing that peace is not only something found externally.
It is also something cultivated internally through the way you speak to yourself, care for yourself, and honor your own well-being.

Many people spend years searching for externally what they have not yet learned to create internally:
safety,
validation,
acceptance,
or compassion.

But healing slowly teaches you how to offer some of those things inwardly instead of constantly abandoning yourself waiting for others to provide them first.

The relationship you have with yourself becomes the emotional foundation beneath your life.

Nurture it gently.

For today, remember this:
The way you treat yourself influences every relationship and experience you carry into your future.

You Are Allowed to Build a Different Kind of Life

Not everyone wants the same things.
Not everyone measures success the same way.
Not everyone is meant to follow identical paths.

And yet, many people spend years trying to force themselves into lives that look acceptable to others while quietly feeling disconnected inside.

Healing often changes this.

You begin asking deeper questions:
What kind of life actually feels healthy to me?
What kind of environment supports my peace?
What rhythms allow me to feel grounded instead of constantly depleted?
What values do I truly want my life to reflect?

These questions matter.

Because a meaningful life is not built through imitation.
It is built through alignment.

You are allowed to create a life that reflects:
your healing,
your priorities,
your values,
your nervous system,
your goals,
and the person you are becoming.

Maybe your life will look quieter than others expected.
Maybe slower.
More intentional.
More peaceful.
Less focused on performance and more focused on sustainability.

Choosing Yourself, One Day At a Time

That does not make your life less meaningful.

There is courage in building a life that genuinely supports your well-being instead of constantly chasing appearances.

Some people will not understand your choices.
They may project their own expectations, fears, or definitions of success onto you.

That is okay.

You are the one who must wake up and live inside your life each day.

You deserve a life that:
supports your peace,
respects your humanity,
allows room for healing,
and feels emotionally sustainable long term.

As you grow, you may become less interested in proving yourself and more interested in living honestly.

That shift changes everything.

Because once you stop organizing your life around external approval, you gain the freedom to build something that actually feels aligned with your spirit.

For today, remember this:
You are allowed to create a life that feels healthy, meaningful, and authentic to you.

You Are Still Becoming Even on the Hard Days

It is easy to believe growth is only happening on the days when you feel motivated, focused, energized, and emotionally strong.

The productive days.
The inspired days.
The breakthrough moments.

But healing is also happening on the difficult days.

The days when you feel uncertain.
The days when emotions feel heavier.
The days when your energy is low.
The days when simply continuing requires effort.

Growth does not disappear just because the process feels hard.

In fact, some of the deepest transformation happens during the seasons where you are quietly learning:
how to stay,
how to endure,
how to soften without giving up,
and how to keep choosing yourself even when life feels emotionally exhausting.

You are still becoming on the days you:
rest instead of self-destruct,
speak kindly to yourself,
ask for support,
set a boundary,
show up imperfectly,
or simply decide not to give up.

These moments matter more than you realize.

Choosing Yourself, One Day At a Time

People often imagine healing as a steady upward climb, but real growth moves in waves. Some days feel clear and hopeful. Other days feel slower and more emotional.

That does not mean you are failing.

It means you are human.

The important thing is not whether every day feels easy.
The important thing is whether you continue returning to yourself with honesty and compassion instead of abandoning yourself completely.

There is strength in continuing gently.

Strength in staying committed to your healing even when progress feels quiet.
Strength in trusting that growth is still unfolding beneath the surface.

Because the truth is, your nervous system, your habits, your mindset, and your emotional world are all learning new ways of existing over time.

That kind of transformation is deep work.

For today, remember this:
You are still growing into yourself, even on the days when the process feels difficult or slow.

Your Peace Is More Valuable Than Winning Every Battle

Not every disagreement deserves your energy.
Not every misunderstanding requires your explanation.
Not every criticism deserves your emotional attention.

As you heal, you begin realizing how exhausting it is to constantly defend yourself, prove yourself, or engage with every source of conflict that enters your life.

You do not have to attend every battle you are invited to.

There is wisdom in learning when to speak and when to step back.
When to clarify and when to let go.
When to protect your peace instead of trying to force understanding from people who are committed to misunderstanding you.

This does not mean becoming passive or avoiding important conversations.
Healthy communication still matters.
Honesty still matters.
Boundaries still matter.

But emotionally healthy people learn discernment.

They learn that constant conflict drains the nervous system.
That proving yourself endlessly rarely creates peace.
That some people are more invested in reaction than resolution.

You are allowed to stop exhausting yourself trying to control every perception people have of you.

Choosing Yourself, One Day At a Time

Not everyone will understand your intentions.
Not everyone will see your growth.
Not everyone will interpret your life accurately.

That is okay.

Your peace matters more than winning every argument.

There is strength in remaining grounded when chaos tries to pull you into emotional exhaustion.
Strength in protecting your energy instead of constantly scattering it trying to manage everyone else's opinions.

Healing often includes learning how to:
pause before reacting,
respond instead of explode,
and walk away from situations that continuously cost you your peace without truly adding value to your life.

A calmer nervous system is worth protecting.

And perhaps one of the most mature realizations is understanding that inner peace often requires letting go of the need to constantly defend your worth, your healing, or your life choices to everyone around you.

For today, remember this:
Protecting your peace is often wiser than trying to win every emotional battle.

You Are Allowed to Build a Life You No Longer Need to Escape

Many people become so accustomed to stress, emotional exhaustion, or survival mode that escape becomes their primary coping mechanism.

Escaping through distraction.
Escaping through overworking.
Escaping through unhealthy habits.
Escaping through fantasy about a completely different life.

But healing slowly shifts your focus.

Instead of constantly asking:
"How do I escape my life?"
you begin asking:
"How do I create a life that feels safer, calmer, and more sustainable to live inside?"

That question changes everything.

Because the goal is not simply temporary relief.
The goal is long-term alignment.

A healthier life is built through repeated choices that reduce internal chaos and increase emotional stability:
better boundaries,
healthier habits,
safer relationships,
financial responsibility,
honest communication,
rest,
discipline,
and self-respect.

This process takes time.

Choosing Yourself, One Day At a Time

You are not rebuilding only your circumstances.
You are rebuilding your relationship with yourself and the environment you create around your mind, body, and spirit.

A life you no longer need to escape from often looks quieter than people expect.

It may include:
steady routines,
peaceful mornings,
honest work,
healthy connection,
rest,
movement,
purpose,
and emotional safety.

Not constant adrenaline.
Not constant performance.
Not constant emotional extremes.

As you heal, you may begin valuing steadiness more than intensity.

That is growth.

You deserve a life where your body can relax.
Where your spirit can breathe.
Where your mind no longer feels trapped in constant survival mode.

It is something you can intentionally build into your everyday life.

For today, remember this:
You are allowed to create a life that feels emotionally safe enough to fully stay present inside.

You Do Not Have to Become Hard to Become Strong

Some people believe strength means becoming emotionally guarded, detached, or hardened by life.

They think healing means no longer feeling deeply.
No longer caring.
No longer being affected.

But true strength is not emotional numbness.

Real strength is remaining open-hearted without constantly abandoning yourself.
It is learning how to care deeply while still protecting your peace.
It is developing boundaries without losing compassion.

Life may try to convince you that softness is weakness.
That vulnerability is dangerous.
That sensitivity should be hidden.

But many of the strongest people are actually the ones who remain kind after hardship.
The ones who continue choosing honesty after disappointment.
The ones who continue loving without losing themselves entirely in the process.

Healing is not about becoming cold.
It is about becoming grounded.

There is a difference.

Choosing Yourself, One Day At a Time

Grounded people feel deeply, but they are no longer controlled by every emotional wave around them.
They know how to pause.
Reflect.
Respond intentionally.
Protect their energy.
And remain connected to themselves even during difficult moments.

You do not need to destroy your tenderness in order to survive this world.

Your softness may actually be part of your strength.

The ability to empathize.
To encourage.
To connect.
To create safe spaces for others.
To remain compassionate without becoming self-sacrificing.

Those qualities matter deeply.

The goal is not to become emotionally unreachable.
The goal is to become emotionally healthy.

Healthy enough to love without self-abandonment.
Healthy enough to care without carrying the entire weight of everyone else's pain.
Healthy enough to remain open while also honoring your own well-being.

For today, remember this:
You do not have to lose your softness in order to become strong.

Your Healing Is Not Linear, and That Is Okay

There may be days when you feel deeply grounded in your growth.

Days when your mind feels clear.
Your habits feel aligned.
Your healing feels visible.

And then there may be days when old emotions return unexpectedly.
Days when exhaustion surfaces.
Days when grief, fear, loneliness, or insecurity suddenly feel louder again.

This does not mean you are moving backward.

Healing moves in layers.

Sometimes growth means revisiting old wounds with new awareness.
Sometimes healing reveals emotions that were buried beneath years of survival mode.
Sometimes your nervous system simply needs more compassion and rest than you expected.

Do not shame yourself for still being human during the process.

Many people assume healing should look like a straight upward line:
constant progress,
constant positivity,
constant clarity.

But real healing is more honest than that.

Choosing Yourself, One Day At a Time

It includes:
setbacks,
uncertainty,
emotional waves,
moments of exhaustion,
and seasons where growth feels quieter and less visible.

That is normal.

The important thing is not whether you feel perfect every day.
The important thing is whether you continue returning to yourself instead of abandoning yourself completely.

Can you pause instead of spiraling?
Can you speak to yourself with compassion instead of shame?
Can you begin again without deciding the entire journey is ruined?

That is healing.

A hard day does not erase your growth.
A difficult season does not erase your progress.
An emotional moment does not erase the healthier life you are building.

Transformation is not measured by never struggling again.
It is measured by your willingness to continue healing honestly instead of pretending you no longer need care.

For today, remember this:
Healing does not need to unfold perfectly in order to be real and meaningful.

You Are Allowed to Believe That Your Life Can Improve

Sometimes pain lasts so long that people begin expecting struggle everywhere.

They stop imagining peace because chaos became familiar.
They stop expecting healthy love because disappointment became familiar.
They stop believing in better possibilities because survival consumed so much of their emotional energy.

But healing asks you to reopen your life to possibility.

Not fantasy.
Not denial.

Possibility.

The possibility that your future can become healthier than your past.
The possibility that your nervous system can experience more peace.
The possibility that your relationships can become safer and more reciprocal.
The possibility that your life can feel more aligned, meaningful, and emotionally sustainable over time.

You are allowed to believe that growth is still available to you.

Not because life will suddenly become perfect, but because human beings are capable of change.

Habits can change.
Mindsets can change.
Patterns can change.
Lives can change.

Choosing Yourself, One Day At a Time

Slowly.
Patiently.
Intentionally.

Many meaningful transformations begin quietly:
a decision to stop abandoning yourself,
a commitment to healing,
a healthier routine,
a difficult boundary,
a return to school,
a prayer whispered in private,
a choice to continue even when progress feels invisible.

Small decisions create different futures.

And perhaps one of the bravest things you can do is continue participating in your own becoming even after difficult seasons tried to convince you to stop believing in yourself.

You do not need every answer right now.
You do not need guaranteed certainty before moving forward.

You only need enough willingness to keep nurturing the healthier life you are trying to create.

Hope is not weakness.
Hope is courage.

For today, remember this:
You are allowed to believe that your future can become healthier, calmer, and more meaningful than your past.

The Life You Want Is Built in Ordinary Moments

People often imagine transformation happening through dramatic breakthroughs.

One perfect decision.
One giant opportunity.
One life-changing moment.

But most meaningful lives are actually built through ordinary moments repeated consistently over time.

The mornings you choose discipline over avoidance.
The evenings you choose rest over self-destruction.
The conversations where you choose honesty over silence.
The small financial choices.
The walks.
The prayers.
The boundaries.
The moments you keep showing up even when no one else sees the effort.

These moments matter.

A peaceful life is rarely created through intensity alone. It is created through rhythms.

Healthy rhythms.
Intentional routines.
Repeated acts of self-respect.

People often overlook ordinary moments because they seem small while they are happening. But years later, those same moments become the foundation beneath an entirely different life.

Choosing Yourself, One Day At a Time

One healthy choice may not feel significant.
But hundreds of healthy choices reshape a person.

Slowly.
Quietly.
Powerfully.

This is why consistency matters more than occasional perfection.

The future is not built only in major milestones.
It is built in the private decisions you continue making when motivation fades and no applause is present.

And perhaps one of the most healing realizations is understanding that you do not need your life to become extraordinary overnight in order for it to become meaningful.

You simply need to continue participating in your own healing, growth, and becoming.

One ordinary moment at a time.

There is beauty in a life built steadily.
Beauty in calm routines.
Beauty in intentional choices.
Beauty in no longer abandoning yourself in the quiet moments where your future is actually being shaped.

For today, remember this:
The ordinary moments you consistently honor today are quietly creating the life you will live tomorrow.

You Are Allowed to Outgrow the Life That Once Fit You

There may have been a time when certain habits, relationships, environments, or dreams made sense for who you were then.

They may have comforted you.
Protected you.
Helped you survive.
Given you identity or belonging during difficult seasons.

But healing changes people.

And sometimes growth means realizing that what once fit you no longer aligns with who you are becoming now.

This can feel bittersweet.

Because outgrowing parts of your old life often comes with grief alongside growth.

You may grieve:
the version of yourself that once settled,
the relationships that no longer feel healthy,
the dreams that changed,
or the environments your spirit no longer feels safe inside.

That grief is normal.

Outgrowing something does not mean it was meaningless.
It simply means you are changing.

Choosing Yourself, One Day At a Time

You are allowed to evolve beyond:
survival mode,
self-abandonment,
chaos,
people-pleasing,
emotional exhaustion,
or patterns that once felt familiar but no longer support your healing.

As you grow, you may begin wanting:
more peace,
more intention,
more honesty,
more emotional safety,
more balance,
and more alignment between your inner life and outer life.

That is not failure.
That is awareness.

Some people will not understand your changes because they only knew older versions of you.

That is okay.

You are not required to remain trapped inside old identities simply because they once felt familiar to others.

The healthiest version of your future may require releasing parts of your past that can no longer travel with you.

That takes courage.

For today, remember this:
You are allowed to outgrow what no longer aligns with the healthier life you are building.

Your Peace Deserves Daily Protection

Peace is not something you create once and never think about again.

It requires maintenance.

Daily choices.
Daily awareness.
Daily boundaries.
Daily honesty with yourself about what nourishes your spirit and what quietly drains it.

Many people work very hard to heal, only to continue allowing environments, habits, or relationships that repeatedly disrupt the peace they are trying to build.

This is why protection matters.

Not fear-based isolation.
Not emotional walls.
But intentional care for your well-being.

Protecting your peace may look like:
getting enough rest,
limiting certain conversations,
stepping away from chaos,
choosing healthier routines,
protecting your time,
saying no more often,
or becoming more selective about who receives access to your emotional energy.

Not everyone will understand this.

Some people are accustomed to the version of you that overextended yourself constantly and ignored your own needs in order to keep everything and everyone else comfortable.

But healing changes your priorities.

You begin realizing that peace is precious.

And once you understand how difficult it was to create more emotional stability within yourself, you naturally become more intentional about protecting it.

Your nervous system matters.
Your emotional well-being matters.
Your inner world matters.

You deserve environments where your body can relax instead of remaining in constant emotional defense.

This does not mean avoiding all discomfort or difficult conversations.
Growth still requires honesty and courage.

But there is a difference between healthy challenge and chronic emotional depletion.

Learning that difference is part of emotional maturity.

And perhaps one of the most healing realizations is understanding that protecting your peace is not selfish — it is necessary for sustaining the healthier life you are building.

For today, remember this:
Your peace deserves consistent care, attention, and protection.

You Are Allowed to Be Proud of How Far You've Come

Sometimes people become so focused on where they still want to go that they forget to honor how much they have already survived, healed, and rebuilt.

They keep moving the finish line.
Keep minimizing their growth.
Keep overlooking the courage it took simply to continue.

But your progress deserves acknowledgment too.

Not because the journey is complete.
Not because you have become perfect.

But because you kept going.

You kept learning.
Kept healing.
Kept rebuilding.
Kept choosing yourself in moments where it would have been easier to give up.

That matters.

You are allowed to feel proud of:
the habits you changed,
the boundaries you learned,
the discipline you practiced,
the healing you committed to,
the peace you protected,
and the healthier life you are slowly creating.

Many transformations happen quietly.

Choosing Yourself, One Day At a Time

No applause.
No dramatic announcement.
Just daily choices repeated over time until one day you realize:
"I am not who I used to be."

That realization deserves tenderness, not dismissal.

Healing often teaches people how to stop defining themselves only by their mistakes, failures, or unfinished goals.

You are more than the areas where you are still growing.

You are also:
your resilience,
your awareness,
your compassion,
your willingness to change,
and your courage to begin again.

The version of you reading this now already carries wisdom that earlier versions of yourself did not yet have.

Do not rush past that truth.

Growth and gratitude can exist together.
Ambition and self-compassion can exist together.
You can still desire more for your future while appreciating how far you have already come.

That balance is healthy.

For today, remember this:
You are allowed to honor the strength, healing, and growth that already exist within your journey.

You Do Not Need to Earn Your Worth Through Exhaustion

Many people learned to measure their worth by how much they could carry.

How productive they were.
How helpful they were.
How much they sacrificed.
How much they endured without falling apart.

So they keep pushing themselves beyond healthy limits trying to prove they are valuable.

They overwork.
Overgive.
Overextend.
Ignore their own needs.
And quietly become emotionally exhausted in the process.

But your worth is not something you have to prove through constant depletion.

You do not become more deserving of love, respect, or rest simply because you exhausted yourself trying to earn it.

Healing often includes unlearning the belief that suffering is what makes you worthy.

You are already worthy while resting.
While healing.
While learning.
While rebuilding.
While still becoming.

This does not mean effort no longer matters.
Effort matters deeply.

But effort rooted in self-respect feels different than effort rooted in self-erasure.

One nourishes growth.
The other drains life from you.

You are allowed to work hard while still caring for your humanity.
You are allowed to pursue goals without abandoning your health.
You are allowed to support others without completely neglecting yourself.

A meaningful life is not sustained by endless exhaustion.

It is sustained by balance.

By rhythms of:
effort and recovery,
discipline and compassion,
ambition and rest.

You deserve a life where your nervous system does not constantly feel like it must prove its value through burnout.

And perhaps one of the most healing realizations is understanding that you no longer need to destroy yourself in order to feel deserving of love, success, or belonging.

You are worthy because you are human.
Not because you exhausted yourself enough to earn permission to matter.

For today, remember this:
Your worth does not increase when you abandon yourself trying to carry everything alone.

You Are Allowed to Choose a Healthier Direction at Any Time

There is no perfect moment required to begin changing your life.

You do not need to wait until everything is figured out.
You do not need to become flawless first.
You do not need permission from the world to begin choosing differently.

You can decide today:
“I want something healthier for my life.”

That decision alone can begin changing your future.

Many people remain stuck because they believe change only “counts” if it happens dramatically. But most meaningful transformation begins quietly.

A healthier routine.
A different boundary.
A new mindset.
A difficult conversation.
A return to school.
A commitment to healing.
A decision to stop abandoning yourself.

Small directional changes matter.

Even if progress feels slow at first, direction is powerful.

One healthier decision repeated consistently can eventually reshape an entire life.

And perhaps one of the most freeing realizations is understanding that your past does not permanently lock you into your future.

Choosing Yourself, One Day At a Time

You are allowed to pivot.
Allowed to rebuild.
Allowed to heal.
Allowed to become more intentional than you once were.

There may be people who only know older versions of you.
There may even be parts of yourself still adjusting to the changes you are trying to create.

That is okay.

Growth often feels unfamiliar before it feels natural.

The important thing is not whether you change perfectly.
The important thing is whether you continue moving toward alignment instead of repeatedly returning to what harms your peace.

Every day presents opportunities to choose again:
peace instead of chaos,
honesty instead of avoidance,
healing instead of self-destruction,
growth instead of hopelessness.

Those choices matter more than you realize.

For today, remember this:
You are always allowed to begin moving your life in a healthier direction.

You Are Becoming More Honest With Yourself

One of the clearest signs of healing is honesty.

Not perfection.
Not performance.
Honesty.

Honesty about what hurts.
What drains you.
What no longer aligns.
What your spirit truly needs.
What patterns continue creating suffering in your life.

For many people, survival required avoidance for a long time.

Avoiding emotions.
Avoiding truth.
Avoiding difficult conversations.
Avoiding the deeper reasons behind unhealthy habits or repeated pain.

And while avoidance may temporarily numb discomfort, it also prevents deeper healing from happening.

Healing asks for honesty instead.

Not harshness.
Not shame.

Just honest awareness.

Choosing Yourself, One Day At a Time

The kind that says:
"This no longer feels healthy for me."
"I cannot keep abandoning myself this way."
"I deserve more peace than this."
"I want a different future."
"I need to care for myself differently now."

These realizations are powerful.

Because once you become honest with yourself, change becomes possible.

You begin noticing:
which relationships feel reciprocal and which feel draining,
which habits support your healing and which sabotage it,
which environments nourish your nervous system and which overwhelm it.

Awareness changes everything.

That does not mean every decision suddenly becomes easy.
Honesty can initially feel uncomfortable because truth often asks you to release familiar patterns that no longer serve your future.

But honesty also creates freedom.

The healthier your relationship with yourself becomes, the harder it becomes to ignore what your heart already knows.

For today, remember this:
Honest self-awareness is one of the most important steps toward lasting healing and peace.

Your Life Is Worth Caring About

Sometimes people become so focused on surviving, helping others, or carrying responsibility that they slowly stop treating their own life as something precious.

They neglect their health.
Ignore their exhaustion.
Dismiss their dreams.
Silence their needs.
Abandon their own well-being while trying to keep everything else functioning.

But your life deserves care too.

Your body deserves care.
Your mind deserves care.
Your spirit deserves care.
Your future deserves care.

You matter beyond what you can provide for other people.

Healing often begins when you stop treating yourself like an afterthought.

When you begin recognizing that:
your peace matters,
your goals matter,
your health matters,
your healing matters,
and the life you are building is worthy of intentional investment.

Choosing Yourself, One Day At a Time

Caring about your life may look like:
going to therapy,
saving money,
resting,
creating healthier routines,
returning to school,
protecting your peace,
ending harmful patterns,
or simply speaking to yourself with more compassion than you once did.

These choices are not selfish.
They are acts of self-respect.

You deserve a life that feels emotionally sustainable and meaningful to live inside.

And perhaps one of the most healing realizations is understanding that caring for yourself is not something you must earn after taking care of everyone else first.

Your humanity already deserves attention and care now.

There is nothing weak about wanting peace.
Nothing selfish about wanting health.
Nothing wrong with wanting your future to become steadier, healthier, and more aligned than your past.

Your life is not a burden to carry reluctantly.
It is something worthy of nurturing intentionally.

For today, remember this:
Your life, healing, and future are worthy of your care, attention, and investment.

You Are Learning How to Stay With Yourself

For many people, difficult emotions immediately trigger the urge to escape.

Escape through distraction.
Through overworking.
Through unhealthy habits.
Through shutting down emotionally.
Through anything that temporarily numbs discomfort.

This often happens because they were never taught how to sit safely with themselves during pain.

But healing changes this relationship slowly.

You begin learning how to stay present with yourself instead of immediately abandoning yourself whenever life feels difficult.

You learn how to pause.
Breathe.
Reflect.
Feel emotions without letting them completely consume your identity.

This is deep work.

Because staying with yourself during difficult moments requires compassion and emotional safety.

It means learning how to say:
"I am struggling right now, but I do not need to destroy myself because of it."
"I can feel this emotion without becoming hopeless."
"I can support myself through this moment."

That is healing.

Choosing Yourself, One Day At a Time

You do not need to become emotionally numb to become emotionally healthy.
You simply need healthier ways of moving through what you feel.

Some emotions will still be uncomfortable.
Grief.
Fear.
Loneliness.
Disappointment.
Uncertainty.

But discomfort is not proof that you are failing.
It is proof that you are human.

The goal is not to avoid all pain forever.
The goal is to become more grounded while moving through it.

And perhaps one of the most beautiful parts of growth is realizing that you no longer completely disappear from yourself during hard seasons.

You stay.
You care for yourself differently.
You speak to yourself more gently.
You continue choosing life, healing, and honesty even while emotions move through you.

That changes everything.

Because a person who learns how to remain connected to themselves during difficult moments becomes much harder for life to completely break.

For today, remember this:
Healing is teaching you how to stay connected to yourself with compassion through every season of life.

You Are Allowed to Build a Life That Reflects Your Healing

As people heal, their lives often begin changing from the inside out.

Not because they are trying to impress others, but because their inner world no longer comfortably aligns with certain patterns, environments, or ways of living.

Healing naturally influences:
how you spend your time,
who you allow close to you,
what habits you practice,
what goals matter to you,
and what kind of life your nervous system can sustainably exist within.

You may begin craving:
more peace,
more honesty,
more rest,
more stability,
more meaningful connection,
and more intentional living.

That is not weakness.
That is alignment.

Your external life eventually begins reflecting the internal work you are doing.

A calmer mind often seeks calmer environments.
Greater self-respect often creates stronger boundaries.
Emotional healing often changes the relationships you are willing to maintain.

This process may feel uncomfortable at times because growth naturally creates change.

Choosing Yourself, One Day At a Time

You may outgrow certain habits.
Certain conversations.
Certain identities.
Even certain dreams.

That is okay.

You are not betraying yourself by evolving.
You are honoring your healing.

Many people try to maintain lives that no longer fit simply because those lives are familiar or socially accepted. But forcing yourself to stay misaligned eventually creates emotional exhaustion.

You deserve a life that reflects the healthier person you are becoming.

A life that supports your peace instead of constantly disrupting it.
A life that nourishes your well-being instead of repeatedly draining it.
A life where your inner healing and outer choices are moving in the same direction.

This does not happen overnight.

It unfolds gradually through repeated intentional decisions.

But every healthy choice you make is helping create a life that feels more emotionally honest and sustainable over time.

For today, remember this:
Your healing is allowed to shape the kind of life you choose to build moving forward.

Your Future Is Being Shaped by What You Practice Today

Every day, whether you realize it or not, you are practicing something.

Practicing self-respect or self-neglect.
Practicing peace or chaos.
Practicing honesty or avoidance.
Practicing discipline or delay.
Practicing healing or repeating old pain.

Over time, what you repeatedly practice becomes the emotional foundation beneath your life.

This is why small daily choices matter so deeply.

A future is not created only through big moments.
It is shaped through repeated patterns.

The way you speak to yourself.
The way you care for your body.
The way you handle stress.
The boundaries you maintain.
The habits you return to when life feels difficult.

These things slowly become your life.

Many people wait for motivation before changing.
But meaningful transformation is often built through practice long before motivation consistently appears.

You practice:
showing up,
beginning again,
staying committed,
and returning to the person you are trying to become even after difficult days.

Choosing Yourself, One Day At a Time

That repetition creates growth.

At first, healthier choices may feel unfamiliar.
Uncomfortable.
Even exhausting.

That is normal.

Your mind, body, and nervous system are learning new ways of existing.

Be patient with yourself during that process.

The important thing is not whether you do everything perfectly.
The important thing is what direction you continue practicing consistently over time.

Because every repeated action strengthens something within you.

Repeated peace strengthens steadiness.
Repeated honesty strengthens alignment.
Repeated care strengthens healing.
Repeated discipline strengthens self-trust.

You are shaping your future through what you repeatedly nurture today.

Choose intentionally.

For today, remember this:
The life you create tomorrow is being practiced through the choices you make today.

You Were Always Worth the Work

Through every difficult season,
every setback,
every beginning again,
every moment you questioned yourself,
every time you carried pain quietly while still trying to keep going —
you were always worthy of healing, peace, growth, and love.

Not once you became perfect.
Not once you achieved enough.
Not once everyone finally approved of you.

Now.

As you are.

This journey was never about becoming someone worthy.
It was about remembering that your humanity already carried worth all along.

The healing.
The boundaries.
The discipline.
The rebuilding.
The honesty.
The forgiveness.
The courage to continue.

All of it mattered.

Not because it made you more valuable, but because it helped reconnect you to the truth that your life deserves care and intention.

Choosing Yourself, One Day At a Time

There will still be seasons ahead.
Still growth.
Still lessons.
Still moments where you must choose yourself again.

But you are no longer the same person who first began this journey.

You have learned:
how to pause,
how to protect your peace,
how to speak to yourself more gently,
how to begin again,
how to survive honestly instead of abandoning yourself completely.

That matters deeply.

And perhaps the most beautiful part of healing is realizing that the life you are building is not rooted in perfection anymore.

You were never behind.
Never broken beyond repair.
Never disqualified from building a meaningful life.

You were always worthy of the work.

Even in the moments you doubted it most.

For today, remember this:
The life, healing, peace, and future you are building are possible because you finally chose to believe that you were worth showing up for.

Closing Reflection

As you come to the end of these pages, pause for a moment.
Take a breath.
Notice where you are now.

Not where you think you should be.
Not where you wish you were.
Just where you are.

Because that is where your life is happening.

This work was never about getting everything right.
It was never about becoming perfect or reaching some final version of yourself.

It was about choosing.

Choosing to show up.
Choosing to be honest.
Choosing to stay with yourself, even when it feels uncomfortable.

And if you've made it here, even in the smallest way—
you have already been doing that.

There will still be days that feel heavy.
Days when old patterns resurface.
Days when you forget everything you've read here.

That does not mean you've failed.
It means you're human.

What matters is not that you never fall back—
but that you are willing to return.

Choosing Yourself, One Day At a Time

Again.
And again.
And again.

You can always begin again.

You can always take a breath.
You can always choose differently.

Not all at once.
But in moments.

And those moments add up.

This is the work.
Quiet. Consistent. Yours.

And through it all, may you remember:

You are not something to fix.
You are someone to choose.

For your growth today, carry this forward.

About The Change Maker

The Change Maker is a personal development platform devoted to growth, healing, and intentional living.

Created by C. Michael Welsh, it was built on a simple belief:
that real change does not happen all at once—it happens in the small, consistent choices we make each day.

Through books, daily reflections, courses, and community, The Change Maker offers a space to slow down, reconnect, and begin again. It is not about becoming someone new, but about returning to who you are beneath the patterns, the pressure, and the expectations that have shaped you.

The work is centered around five core areas of life:

Change — embracing growth and the courage to evolve
We Do Recover — honoring the journey of healing and renewal
Parenthood — leading with presence, patience, and love
Leadership — showing up with integrity, purpose, and heart
Consciousness — deepening awareness and connection to self

Each offering is designed to meet you where you are—not with judgment, but with understanding. Not with pressure, but with possibility.

Because the life you are building is shaped in the choices you make today.

Just for today.

About the Author

C. Michael Welsh is a writer, speaker, and creator of THE CHANGE MAKER—a personal development platform devoted to helping others grow, heal, and live with intention.

His work is deeply rooted in lived experience. Through his own journey of overcoming adversity, navigating recovery, and learning to choose himself one day at a time, Michael has developed a grounded and compassionate approach to personal transformation. Since August 30, 2022, he has remained committed to sobriety and to building a life centered in clarity, presence, and purpose.

Michael’s professional background is in talent acquisition, where he has built a career helping individuals find meaningful work and supporting organizations in developing strong, connected teams. He holds a Master’s Certificate in Human Resource Management with a focus on Diversity and Inclusion from Cornell University, and his work reflects a deep commitment to equity, belonging, and the belief that every person deserves the opportunity to succeed.

Through THE CHANGE MAKER, Michael extends that mission beyond the workplace—creating books, courses, and daily reflections designed to meet people where they are and support them in becoming who they are meant to be. His writing blends personal insight with practical reflection, offering a steady and approachable path for those seeking growth, healing, and direction in their lives.

At the heart of his work is a clear purpose:
to help others recognize their worth, reconnect with

themselves, and take intentional steps toward a more aligned and meaningful life.

Michael's HEART OF… series and his broader body of work are built on the belief that transformation is not something that happens all at once—it is created through small, consistent choices made over time.

Not through perfection.
But through presence.

And through a willingness to do the work.

Made in the USA
Monee, IL
12 November 2026

b4c708c8-b216-4e5a-8e97-9e3a65d74442R01